D1265119

THEODORE ROOSEVELT

THE MAN AS I KNEW HIM

Also by Nicholas Roosevelt

A FRONT ROW SEAT

A NEW BIRTH OF FREEDOM

CREATIVE COOKING

THEODORE ROOSEVELT

THE MAN AS I KNEW HIM

By Nicholas Roosevelt

ILLUSTRATED WITH PHOTOGRAPHS

DODD, MEAD & COMPANY · NEW YORK

Library of Congress Catalog Card Number: 67-13368

Printed in the United States of America
by Vail-Ballou Press, Inc., Binghamton, N. Y.

ACKNOWLEDGMENTS

I AM INDEBTED to two of Theodore Roosevelt's children, Ethel (Mrs. Richard Derby) and Archie, for helpful suggestions and for verification of personal recollections. Close ties with them since childhood have kept alive my early devotion and admiration for their father and mother. I am particularly grateful to them for reminding me of persons whom TR had known well and whose opinions he valued. Many of these persons I also knew well.

To Miss Helen MacLachlan of the Theodore Roosevelt Association I owe thanks for helpful leads and for the checking of quotations, the verification of names and dates, and for placing books at my disposal through which I could compare my own recollections with printed records.

Among sources of hitherto unpublished material I am grateful to the Henry E. Huntington Library in Pasadena, California, for permission to use notes made by the one-time director of that library, Dr. Max Farrand, about TR's account of the Panama incident. I am also grateful to Mr. J. C. Greenway and the Arizona Historical Society for permission to use material in the Greenway collection in Tucson.

Two old friends among American historians, Allan Nevins, formerly of the faculty of Columbia University, and Edgar E. Robinson, for years head of the Institute of American History at Stanford University, were kind enough to read the manuscript in process and made helpful suggestions about contents and additional source material for verification, for which I am grateful.

I am also indebted to three friends for meticulous proofreading: Mrs. Edgar Leaycraft, Mrs. Melissa Blake Levitzky, and Mrs. Betty Tolerton. It was my good fortune to have the copying of the manuscript in the competent hands of Mrs. Helen M. Hughes, who was skilled in deciphering textual changes which I had inserted in my illegible handwriting.

NICHOLAS ROOSEVELT

Big Sur, California

FOREWORD

NICHOLAS ROOSEVELT presents his sheaf of recollections, observations, and judgments concerning TR with modesty, as befits an onlooker who played no part in the great public transactions of the time with which he deals. His book nevertheless has two unique qualities that give it significance. It embodies the memories of a keen-eyed and impressionable youth passing from adolescence into young manhood, the very type in whom TR took the liveliest interest. A warm sympathy enabled them to speak to each other without reserve. The book also embodies the more mature impressions of a man who, while a member of the Roosevelt family circle, was enough of a journalist, office-holder, and historian to view the chief member of that family, dazzling though he sometimes was, with critical objectivity. TR walked in an atmosphere of unending controversy. Some honest men hated him as fiercely as others loved him. Looking at him through eyes of family appreciation, Nicholas Roosevelt nevertheless saw all his limitations and many of his faults, and sets them down candidly.

We can never know too much about the personality of Theodore Roosevelt. Out of the smoke and confusion, the sensational headlines and frothy enthusiasm of the brief war with Spain, he sprang as the first national leader in a half century to combine energy, courage, and imagination. The tawdry little conflict conferred a number of quite unanticipated benefits upon a country too long gripped by Drift and Privilege. It destroyed yellow fever; it blazoned the necessity for an isthmian canal and a navy to move through it; it gave Georgia and New York a reborn comradeship; it imparted to millions their first glimmer of world opportunities and responsibilities; in fifty departments it quickened the tempo of life; and as sign and seal of a new era it projected Theodore Roosevelt to a seat where he could define harsh new tasks, arouse new determinations, and start reaping new rewards.

Nicholas Roosevelt discovered this challenging, disconcerting personality as the country discovered him. Both discovered Roosevelt's power of dramatizing himself and his policies, sometimes bumptiously and arrogantly—"I took Panama"; his demands upon courage and love of combat—"Hit the line hard; don't foul and don't shirk, but hit the line hard"; his unending restless energy, "half St. Paul and half St. Vitus," said John Morley; his scorn of frauds and shufflers, and his ability to impale them on a phrase—"Byzantine logothetes"; his interest in everything, so that he was unable to look at a ship without citing a line in Herodotus, or to stride across a lawn without picking up a feather and surmising that the orioles were migrating two weeks earlier than usual; his marvelous memory, that Macaulay's own nephew said equalled Macaulay's; perhaps above all his intense vitality, that made other men look a little pallid, and that, tiring friends, sometimes tired the country.

What an incomparable friend for a growing boy!—and Nicholas Roosevelt enables us better than other writers to realize the fact. Himself, as one critic put it, a "boy eternal," TR loved all games, especially outdoors; he tried to drag Cabinet members into hide and seek; he organized picnics and clambakes; he soaked the children on strenuous hikes; he taught everybody to shoot at targets; he liked rowing, which was vigorous, but eschewed sailing, which wasn't; and when momentarily sedentary, could entertain a circle with horrendous ghost stories.

Did he fry the steaks, as Nicholas avers, or boil them in grease, as Archie declared?—at any rate, he cooked them. All the while he called up pictures of the storied past, especially the "hero-stories" on which he wrote a book; and charted plans for a lifetime of effort, as in his first annual message he drew a map for national growth in his two administrations. As we read these pages we can understand why William Hard wrote that TR's mind was a prism that turned cold prosaic landscapes into bright rainbow vistas. We can understand why William Allen White wrote: 'He poured into my heart such visions, such ideals, such hopes, such a new attitude toward life and patriotism and the meaning of things, as I had never dreamed men had."

From long observation and from family confidences Nicholas Roosevelt is able to tell us much that is new and revealing about the two wives who brightened TR's life, Alice Lee briefly and Edith Carow with lifelong devotion and aid. His parents as always remain mysterious; particularly his father, who impressed contemporaries as a model civic leader but remains quite unlimned. But we would search long to find so discerning an impression of Edith Carow, rich in poise, intelligence, and tact. Equally discerning are the author's pictures of TR's sisters: the volatile, mercurial, enthusiastic Corinne, and the keen-minded, downright, and at times tart Bamie. All three women not only loved TR but admired him to the point of adulation; all were possessive; and all three had strong individual tastes. Some friction was inevitable, but it was in Bamie's home that after TR's funeral his widow sought refuge and solace. Upon the sons the author is less revealing. But in his spirited account of a hunting trip with TR in the Grand Canyon habitat of the Navajos, just after the Convention of 1912, a narrative studded with vivid passages from his diary, he projects Archie and Quentin into the background. TR himself, in this last summer of rugged health—the summer before he departed on his disastrous Brazilian adventure—characteristically occupies the foreground.

Readers interested in political history will value some of the fresh details to be found in Nicholas Roosevelt's stirring record, again taken largely from his diary, of his train journey with TR to the Republican Convention of 1912, and the tumultuous days that followed. TR took Ferrero along and read Roman politics as a preparatioon for meeting the steam roller tactics of Elihu Root and the National Committee. Much more illuminating than new political facts on the triumph of the bosses, and the revolt of the Progressives, is the continued light thrown on TR's personality. Always resilient and hopeful, he remained cheerful throughout the bludgeoning he received. The author is able to declare just what other intimates asserted: "he never lost his dignity, his good humor, and his fighting spirit." When he returned to Oyster Bay certain of defeat that fall by Woodrow Wilson he was still brightly cheerful. Three facts sustained him—the prospect of another good fight; his confidence that he would far outrun Taft (he delighted in estimating just how few electoral votes Taft would get); and his belief that he was founding a new Opposition dedicated to reform and regeneration.

The author's estimates of TR's associates in politics and government are arresting because they spring in part from TR himself, and in part from sources close to him. They contain some unexpected judgments—a more generous treatment of Henry Cabot Lodge, by far, than most observers in any party would endorse; an attribution to Gifford Pinchot of a broader statesmanship than is customarily assigned him; and the inclusion among TR's really influential advisors of Emlen Roosevelt, who was valued for his austere rectitude and expertness in finance. Much of the value of this interesting, informative, and ably written book lies in such unexpected passages. Not at all unexpected is its treatment of Woodrow Wilson, who belonged too vitally to another church, another faith, and another outlook to be regarded amiably. The author has provided a great body of material that nobody else could have furnished, and has done it with zest and objectivity.

Allan Nevins

CONTENTS

ILLUSTRATIONS

Following page 112

(All photographs courtesy of the Theodore Roosevelt Association)

ILLUSTRATIONS

THEODORE ROOSEVELT

THE MAN AS I KNEW HIM

1

IN PERSPECTIVE

THE TIME was noon, July 3, 1898. The place, my mother's summer home at Oyster Bay on the North Shore of Long Island. The exact spot: the top of a bluff above the bay, at the end of a dirt path leading from the house. I had had my fifth birthday three weeks before—the youngest of three children surviving out of five. Contemporary photographs show a sullen brat with long golden curls and inky eyes as irreverent as they were observant.

As my brother and I, under Mother's watchful care, busied ourselves filling small pails with sand on this third day of July, a house guest ran down the path waving a newspaper and calling out that the Rough Riders had taken San Juan Hill in Cuba and that Theodore Roosevelt was being hailed as a national hero. Of course I did not know what San Juan Hill was or anything more about the Rough Riders than that our neighbor and cousin, Theodore, had something to do with them. But I sensed my mother's enthusiasm and excitement, unaware that TR's exploit would affect my entire life as a result of the world prominence that he was bringing to the family name. Four months later he was elected governor of New York, and on September 14, 1901, at the age of forty-two, he became President of the United States.

Because of Theodore's devotion to my father, J. West Roosevelt, who had died in 1896 at the age of thirty-seven and who had been a close friend of his since early childhood (they were first cousins, the sons of brothers), TR showed a special friendliness for me. In my youth I saw much of him and of his four younger children, Kermit, Ethel, Archie, and Quentin. I swam with him, rode with him, shot with him, ate food that he had cooked, listened to him read, heard him quote poetry, and talk about books that he had read and liked and about political figures, past and contemporary, at home and abroad—about Lincoln, who was one of his great heroes as was Andrew Jackson, and about Thomas Jefferson, whom he regarded with picturesque distaste, and many others. I heard him being interviewed by the press, read drafts of speeches he was planning to make, and best of all heard him hold forth as host at Sagamore Hill and in the White House to all manner of guests, foreign and domestic, and draw them into vigorous talk on national and international affairs. I went with TR to the Republican National Convention in Chicago in 1912 and later that year worked at the Progressive Party headquarters in New York. In 1913 he asked me to join him and his sons Archie and Quentin camping and hunting in northern Arizona. When, in 1914, I went to Europe as a young attaché at the American Embassy in Paris, he gave me letters of introduction to persons who could be of help or interest. During 1916 and '17, when I had returned home, I saw him frequently and he spoke to me at length about the likelihood that the United States would be forced into World War I and the urgent need to strengthen the nation's defenses. When he died I was in my twenty-sixth year—a captain in World War I and at that moment assigned on a mission to Austria-Hungary for the American Commission to Negotiate Peace. I doubt if any Roosevelt of my generation saw so much of him as I did, except his own children.

Hence this book. It is neither biography nor history, but rather a combination of personal recollections and impressions based on diaries, letters, and memory and on much reading about the man and his times. During the years in which I saw him so often I shared the devotion that all felt for him who knew him well. But I hope that my life work as journalist and author and occasional member of government missions has given me a sufficient background of national and international affairs to enable me to appraise TR without too much personal bias and yet with the advantage of having known the man well, which so many historians and biographers who have written about him lacked.

Born before the Civil War, TR matured in a nation that was still split sectionally and stratified socially—a nation of rugged individualists changing from an economy based on agriculture, manpower, and animals into an industrialized society in which machines were replacing muscles and corporate directors were displacing individual initiative. In 1880 half the nation's workers were listed as engaged in agriculture. By 1900 the proportion had dropped to a quarter. Life toward the end of the nineteenth century was simple and, compared to modern standards, uncomfortable. Many communities had no running water for household use. In 1900 only a tiny percentage of homes in the United States were serviced with electricity. Lighting was still largely by kerosene and candle, and in the larger cities by gas. In 1900 only eight thousand automobiles were registered in the United States. Twenty years later there were ten million. Home telephones were rare in 1900. By 1920 they were plentiful. Food in all but the high-priced restaurants was often unhealthy because of poor methods of preservation. The sixty-hour week was widespread, and wages were low. The living quarters of the poor were shockingly crowded and insanitary, on a par with the worst slums in Europe. The gulf between the "haves" and the "have-nots" was great—especially in the cities. Society was almost as rigid in the United States as in Victorian England, and the influence of the rich on politics as great or greater here than there. In fact, government in the United States was tending more and more to become a plutocracy.

With the growth of big corporations and business and financial combinations after the Civil War the attitude of businessmen toward politics became increasingly cynical. While corruption was rife in both parties the Republican Party, which, in its early days, was regarded as a party of liberal protest against political reaction, became the tool of big business. Except for TR's seven and a half years in the White House the Republican Party has remained the party of extreme conservatism ever since the death of Abraham Lincoln. Now and then in a few states—Wisconsin in 1898, Oregon in 1900, Iowa in 1902, Kansas in 1904, and California under Governor Hiram Johnson in 1910, are cases in point—the party showed liberal trends. But in national affairs it has been the haven of foes of change and progress and the hope of all whose philosophy of government and society centered on turning back the hands of the clock.

To TR the alliance of business and politics presented not only a challenge but also an opportunity. The challenge was to fight corruption. The opportunity was, in so doing, to dramatize himself as the champion of reform. Not only was he rendering a much-needed service in fighting bribery in government on the part of big businessmen and corporations, but he was stressing needed reforms that could only be achieved by enlarging the powers of government to regulate working conditions, hours of labor, compensation for injury, and many other by-products of the process of industrialization. He saw that only the federal government could perform these functions effectively. In time he advocated income and estate taxes and many forms of impingement on the traditional rights of the individual to be free from any kind of interference on the part of government of any level.

As is made plain in the chapter "Pragmatic Reformer" TR was an early advocate of political and economic controls which were later adopted—some not until his distant kinsman, Franklin D. Roosevelt, succeeded to the presidency. The platform of the

Progressive Party that nominated TR for President in 1912 after the Republican Party had denied him the nomination has a distinct "New Deal" flavor. But important as was his encouragement of progressive theories of government I think that his impact in this field is less significant than his unceasing fight for higher standards in government and for the cognate goal of applying to big business the same ethical standards expected of the average small man in business. This was at the root of his campaign for a "square deal"—which meant equality of treatment as well as of opportunity for all. By the success of his own career in politics he also did much to raise the level of respect in which politicians were held and to inspire young men to take a more active part in politics.

It is one of the paradoxes of TR's career that he, who saw things so clearly, found it hard to sense how unyielding was the enmity of the conservatives toward him. This was based, perhaps in part, on the fact that many of those who criticized him most bitterly were clubmates or social acquaintances whom he liked personally. Because of his instinctive kindness it was, I am sure, hard for him to see that the very fact of their ties of friendship with him made his policies seem to them all the more reprehensible. They felt that he was letting them down, that he was "betraying his class." A remark attributed to the elder J. P. Morgan when someone asked him jokingly when TR went to Africa in 1909 if he, Mr. Morgan, did not mourn TR's absence for a year, illustrates the intensity of their feelings: "All true Americans ought to rejoice in his absence," said the formidable Wall Street financial ruler, "and I sincerely hope that it will be extended indefinitely. He will go down in history as the man who caused incalculable injury to the country."[1] TR, in turn, looked on his conservative business friends as amiable and not very intelligent persons who were unable to understand the changes in American public life.

In the light of my own fifty years of observing and writing

about the American political scene I believe that TR's failure to realize the intensity of the opposition to him on the part of reactionary Republicans was the basis of his major political errors. I have in mind particularly his statement on election night in 1904 that under no circumstances would be accept another nomination for the presidency—a statement that played directly into the hands of his enemies—and his attempt in 1912 to win the Republican nomination for that office. It is conceivable that he would have fought as hard in 1912 had he understood the grim determination of the reactionaries to wreck the Republican Party if necessary to prevent his nomination. But had he fully realized this he might well have been less inclined to be swayed by the ineluctable fact that he was the choice of the majority of the Republican voters—from which he made the delusive deduction that his obvious strength as a vote-getter gave him a fighting chance to win the nomination. He failed to see that the very fact that he had such great popular strength hardened the G.O.P. leaders to prevent his nomination. If he returned to power, their own influence in the party would be greatly curtailed.

I question whether TR can be termed a master politician—by which I mean skilled in getting other politicians to implement his political objectives. The fact that he, an ardent progressive, picked William Howard Taft as his successor in the White House—a man whose inclinations and personal affiliations were close to the reactionary Republican leaders with whom TR had so bitterly fought—is a reflection either on his political sagacity or his judgment of men, or both. But TR's great political strength lay in his millions of devoted followers, especially in rural and small-town America. In a sense he was the first truly national political hero, rather than the idol of merely a section. Since the death of Lincoln, which had occurred only thirty-six years before TR became President, no holder of that office had aroused much enthusiasm. Grant, great as a general, was a poor President. Hayes, Arthur, Harrison, and McKinley were accepted as kindly but colorless worthies. Even the sturdy and able Cleveland was admired rather than loved. But TR aroused great enthusiasm, not only because of his skill in dramatizing his actions and phrasing his aspirations for the country, but also because of his fearlessness, his good humor, and his good sense. He combined the dramatic talents of an expert showman with the moral zeal of a revivalist preacher and the combativeness of a compulsive reformer.

Of his domestic policies the most significant was his concern about conservation. When he took office millions of acres of public lands were unsurveyed and only little explored; other millions were being exploited and plundered illegally by lumber, mining, and grazing interests. Such supervision as the federal government exercised over the public lands that it nominally controlled was performed by political hacks who were scantily paid, inadequately checked, and who devoted as little time as possible to the performance of their duties for the federal government. TR made it one of his earliest concerns to have the public lands surveyed and classified and their use planned and policed with the broad objectives of preserving forests for long-range use, preventing over-grazing, and developing irrigation and water power, as well as opening up to homesteading such parts of the public domain as were suited to agriculture. Little had been done along these lines before he became President. When he left the White House the influence of predatory individuals and corporations again came to the fore.

Because he was President in quiet times his record does not place him on a par with Lincoln and Washington. Yet he was a successful President who achieved much in that office. He received the Nobel peace prize for his part in ending the Russo-Japanese War in 1905. Shortly thereafter, when a crisis in world affairs arose as a result of the German Emperor William's attempt to carve out a German sphere of influence in North

Africa, TR quietly but actively helped in the calling of what came to be known as the Algeciras Conference, usually credited with having played an important part in postponing the outbreak of World War I, which, in 1906, seemed imminent. No other President except John Quincy Adams had such a thorough knowledge of world affairs as did TR, and, more even than Adams, Roosevelt understood the role of sea power in international relations.

As I show in the two final chapters, TR's part in awakening the American people to the influence of the world crisis on the United States in the years before the United States entered the First World War stands out as the greatest single contribution that he made to American history. The odds against him were almost hopeless. Tradition, ignorance, apathy, self-righteousness, short-term self-interest, false optimism, procrastination—these American attitudes between 1914 and 1917 were tolerated by a President who knew little of world affairs and who was averse to exerting leadership. The American people in these years were lulled and deluded into thinking that they could at the same time remain neutral and unarmed and yet could induce nations engaged in a desperate struggle for national survival to knuckle under to the demands of the American government to respect the rights of American citizens. It fell to Theodore Roosevelt to lead the fight for the one thing that alone could affect the outcome of the war and that, if started soon enough and pushed hard enough, might even have made it unnecessary for the United States to become a belligerent—the campaign to increase greatly the naval and military strength of the United States. When TR began his fight for preparedness the President and most of Congress were adamantly opposed to it, as were nearly all the newspapers in the country. The administration for months contented itself with a Micawber-like policy of hoping that something would turn up that would make it unnecessary to face this unpopular choice. By the time that Germany had forced us into the war TR's persistence, coupled with the compelling force of the arguments in favor of preparedness, had done much to educate the American people to the inevitability of involvement in the war.

For those who are vague about dates: TR was born on October 27, 1858; graduated from Harvard College in 1880, and in October of that year married Alice Hathaway Lee, of Chestnut Hill, Massachusetts. He was elected to the New York State Assembly in 1881 and served in that body through 1884, having been nominated for speaker but defeated in 1882. He headed the New York delegation to the Republican National Convention in 1884. Two years later he was nominated for mayor of New York and defeated. In December, 1886, he married Edith Kermit Carow, his first wife, Alice Lee, having died two years previously. From 1889 through 1895 he served as Civil Service Commissioner in Washington, and then was for two years Police Commissioner of New York City. In April, 1897, President McKinley appointed him Assistant Secretary of the Navy. He resigned from that office to help form the Rough Rider regiment of volunteers in the war with Spain. On his return from the war in 1898 he was nominated and elected governor of New York, and in 1900, against his inclination, was nominated for Vice-President and elected to that office. He succeeded to the presidency on the death of William McKinley on September 14, 1901, and was elected President in his own right in 1904, serving until March 4, 1909.

This finished his official career—five months after his fiftieth birthday. He then went to Africa to hunt big game and on his way home early in 1910 made a tour of Europe. In 1912 he contended unsuccessfully for the Republican nomination for President, but became the candidate of the newly formed Progressive Party for that office. In the November elections in 1912 he ran ahead of Taft, but lost to Woodrow Wilson. In the autumn of 1913 he went to South America on a hunting and exploring expedition, returning in the spring of 1914. Shortly after the start of World War I he began a vigorous campaign to arouse the country to the need of military preparedness. When the United States entered the war in 1917 he asked to be allowed to raise and take a division of volunteers to Europe, which request was refused. Throughout the latter part of 1918 he was hospitalized for two long periods, and on January 6, 1919, almost two months after the Armistice, he died in his sleep at Oyster Bay.

2

CHILDREN'S HERO

My earliest recollections of TR go back to summers at Oyster Bay, at the turn of the century, when sixteen children of Roosevelt cousins spent much of their time playing together. All but one of the sixteen were born between 1883 and 1894. I was among the three youngest. We liked nothing better than to have TR as leader in group games and outings. To be with him was to have fun, if for no other reason than that he so obviously was having a good time himself. As Lincoln Steffens aptly phrased it: "The gift of the gods to Theodore Roosevelt was joy—joy in life." He loved to play, but he also loved his work, and in both he applied literally the injunction in the Book of Ecclesiastes: "Whatsoever thy hand findeth to do, do it with thy might." We knew that TR scorned cowardice, meanness and evasiveness and that he expected obedience. But we also knew that he was scrupulously fair and that he would even intercede in our behalf when our mothers took a dim view of our conduct if he thought that we deserved it. This, of course, strengthened our feeling that even though he was one of the grownups he was at heart our friend and ally.

Just as children loved TR, so he loved children—his own, their cousins, his grandchildren, all children. The mothers often chided him (but gently!) for picking up a sleeping baby and cuddling it. As soon as a child learned to walk he would solemnly accompany it hand-in-hand on adventurous journeys about the nursery or in the garden, and as the children grew older he went through a regular romping ritual with each, including pillow fights and playing bear. Even those of us who were very young were struck by his irrepressible cheerfulness and by his genuine interest in each of his young relatives.

During the summer it was the custom at Sagamore Hill for his children and any of their cousins who happened to be there at mealtime to eat with the grownups, which often meant that we would sit down with a member of the cabinet or a foreign ambassador or some other distinguished visitor. In theory we children were supposed to listen rather than talk—but listening has always been hard for my Roosevelt relatives, who are never happier than when a group of them meet and all talk at the same time, deaf or indifferent to what the others are saying. But even the youthful Roosevelts would stop talking when TR took the floor, because his conversation was so dynamic and his humor so explosive. I do not recall his ever using any kind of profanity. In its stead he coined epithets that gained force because of their picturesqueness. I remember his characterizing Root's part in the stealing of delegates at the Republican Convention in 1912 as that of a "modern Autolycus—'A snapper-up of unconsidered trifles.' " (The phrase is from Shakespeare's *The Winter's Tale.*) Owen Wister, after talking with TR in December, 1914, about the causes that led the Germans to declare war, quoted TR as asking speculatively: "How many lies do you suppose that Viennese Christmas-tree jumping jack told that male prima donna at Potsdam?" (the "Christmas-tree jumping jack" being the Austrian Emperor, Franz Josef, and the "male prima donna at Potsdam" being the German Kaiser, William II).[1] John Hay noted in his diary after a cabinet meeting that TR had received a letter asking if he wanted to annex any more islands and had answered: "About as much as a gorged anaconda wants to swallow a porcupine wrong end to."[2] When he used phrases such as these he often bit off the words and spoke them with deliberate overemphasis, usually grinning or laughing as he did so.

The meals at Sagamore Hill stand out particularly vividly in my memory because they were so frequent, through the years, and so full of fun and interest. The fare was always simple but plentiful; and while he was in no sense a gourmet, he was a hearty eater. Eating was, in fact, one of his few forms of self-indulgence. When his wife chided him, as she often did, for taking substantial second helpings he would quote with glee a remark that he had read: "I'm not hungry, but thank God I'm greedy!" which always drew tart, even though affectionate, disapproval from Edith. Heavy eating, in happy ignorance of calories and vitamins, was traditional in those days, but TR differed from his overweight contemporaries in that he practiced the kind of strenuous physical life that he preached, with much walking and riding all year and rowing and chopping in summer. When we were in Arizona in the summer of 1913 his waist was larger than his chest—and his chest was powerful and well-developed. Although he stood only five feet eight inches his large frame and thick neck gave the impression of a big man. This impression was intensified by his habit of standing with his shoulders well thrown back. I do not have any record of his weight in his later years, but when he was in the White House it was over two hundred pounds.

Not until we were in our teens did we begin to be aware of his great courage and self-control. When we were old enough to compare him consciously with others we saw that the quickness of his mind and the retentiveness of his memory were phenomenal. By then we knew that he was a master in guiding public opinion, but we had not learned that from the start of his political career the year after he graduated from Harvard he had displayed an extraordinary talent for leadership. In retrospect the bare record is hard to believe: at the age of twenty-three, nominated for speaker of the New York State Assembly by the

Republicans, who were in the minority; at twenty-five, leader of the New York state delegation to the Republican National Convention in Chicago; at twenty-eight nominated for mayor of New York City on the Republican ticket—all in spite of the fact that in those days he was regarded as brash and bumptious and still shared the nineteenth century concept of a class-conscious society.

When TR joined our games he did so with gusto, and I think that often he enjoyed them as much—or even more—than we did. His close friend, Owen Wister, was right in insisting that deep in him was what Shakespeare called the "boy eternal." In rainy weather our favorite game, in which he happily took part, was hide-and-seek in the Old Barn. This barn no longer stands. Its frame was made of heavy hand-hewn beams of white oak, almost a foot in width, that bound the sides of the barn together and held up the roof. The hay usually was piled somewhat higher than the first tier of crossbeams, with the result that under each beam was a tunnel through which small boys easily scrambled, to be followed (not so easily) by the rather stout President of the United States cheerfully trying to force his way through passages that even some of the older children found tight. It was characteristic of TR's boyishness and sense of fun that he liked to try to induce a member of his cabinet or other visiting dignitary to join in these games—and such was his persuasiveness that a few succumbed despite the sticky heat of a wet Long Island summer day. The only cabinet member whom I clearly remember joining in these games was the Attorney General, William H. Moody, but I am sure that if TR could have induced the austere and wiry Secretary of State, Elihu Root, or the somewhat pompous and paunchy Senator Chauncey M. Depew or Ambassador Joseph H. Choate to join us, he would have done so with glee.

Picnics were also a major diversion in hot weather. Usually they were at Eel Creek on the Cold Spring Harbor side of the

Theodore Roosevelt property, which could only be reached on foot, everybody carrying baskets with equipment and food. The greatest attraction of the picnics, culinarily speaking, was a clambake. This was done according to the traditional New England and Long Island procedure: A flat-bottomed hole was dug in the sand and lined with seaweed. On this bed of seaweed the clams (known on Long Island as "hard-shells" and in New England as "quahogs") were placed with the hinge in the shell resting on the seaweed. Over the clams went more seaweed, and then a bed of embers. The heat from the coals penetrated through the soggy seaweed, effectively steaming the clams. Usually the clams were well seasoned with sand, and often overcooked and therefore tough as leather. They were accompanied by hard-boiled eggs and sandwiches and washed down with lukewarm ginger ale. Part of the family tradition is the story that Archie, perhaps six, on his first encounter with a clam, went through a picnic lunch of eggs and sandwiches in, for him, unusual silence and at the end of the meal turned to his father and asked: "What do I do now with the little dead clam?"

Another of the best-loved group activities was cross-country hiking. TR was the leader, and it was part of the fun—and, without our knowing it, the discipline—that each child followed the leader in single file. This meant that if TR climbed over a large log or waded through a stream or muddy pond it was up to each youngster to do as he did, without evasion or complaint. We loved it, although the mothers disapproved, particularly when we came home soaked. It was after a chilling autumn hike that Mrs. Roosevelt decreed, on seeing her wet brood, that all had to be dosed with a bitter drug then thought to be a cold preventive. The tradition is that Kermit, perhaps ten or twelve years old, went to his father and ruefully said: "*She* says that I've got to take the stuff. Can't *you* do something to stop her?" To which TR is reputed to have replied: "Kermit, I'll be lucky if *she* doesn't make *me* take it also!" How the other Roosevelt parents felt about his soaking us on a hike may be judged from the fact that on one such occasion my mother, who could be tart when mad, upbraided my sister, who had been on the hike, for getting wet. When my sister tried to exculpate herself by explaining that she was simply following her cousin Theodore, who was the leader, my mother said to her sharply: "Just because your cousin Theodore behaves like an *idiot* is no reason why *you* should behave like an idiot."

TR took special delight in chopping trees, even though he was not agile with an ax. It was characteristic of him that if a stranger appeared while he chopped, he would explain that he was engaged in "beavering" the tree. But he "beavered" with vigor, and we youngsters were as happy to be with him thinning trees as we were to play games in the Old Barn or to go on picnics.

As we grew older we were permitted first to watch target practice and then to take part in it. He had a small rifle range in a safe hollow and not only kept up his own skill as a marksman, which was considerable, but also taught us youngsters how to shoot. We began with a .22, and, if I remember rightly, progressed to a 30–30. He gave us detailed instructions about the care and handling of guns, the sighting and aiming, and, above all, the manners of the rifle range. He warned us against ever pointing a gun, whether loaded or not, at anyone, anywhere, any time. Among the few recollections I have of his showing sharpness toward any of us youngsters was if someone was careless with a weapon. I have often thought how right he was to impress on us so deeply the importance of this basic practice.

As the years passed we spent long hours on the tennis court. He was not a good player, but he loved the game and relished the exercise, especially on hot days. During the summer of 1912—the year of the split in the Republican Party that resulted in the formation of the Progressive Party with him as candidate for President—one of Archie's and my assignments (he was eighteen and I was nineteen) was to be ready to play with TR and a fourth, whenever he could get an hour off from his appointments. The tennis court was in a shady hollow about five hundred yards from the house on Sagamore Hill. Callers would usually be given the choice of waiting in the cool house until he came back or of walking down through the hot hayfield to the tennis court to watch until the day's match ended.

Unlike the other Roosevelts of his generation, TR never cared for sailing, but he loved to row. I suspect that the reason for this was that it was a good form of exercise for his vigorous frame and that it gave him a chance to be with his wife without other company. Many days each summer the two spent hours alone on Cold Spring Harbor, eating their lunch on the beach, happily free from the intrusion of curiosity seekers.

When we went on overnight camping trips, which were for boys only, Archie and I usually went with him as steersmen. The two of us would huddle in the stern, comfortable and happy at the prospect of the camping trip, while he, rowing vigorously, was equally happy—but far from comfortable because of the heat of Long Island's summer afternoons. Many is the hour that I spent as a small boy watching the sweat drip from his square forehead, nose and straggly moustache as he pulled the short, quick strokes of a skilled oarsman. Sometimes he rowed in silence, but he was always glad to talk with us about what we had been doing or books we were reading or things that concerned him.

Our favorite overnight camping place was known as Fox Point, on the Sound side of Lloyd's Neck. At this spot there was a good stretch of beach and a flat place behind the dunes with plenty of driftwood for the campfire. Under his supervision we followed a fixed routine: drawing up the unloaded boats (the older boys had come by themselves) out of reach of the tide and carrying food and blankets to the campground; gathering wood; staking out each youngster's sleeping spot; then, weather and tide (and TR) permitting, we stripped and swam in the Sound. The older boys then started the fire, and when it was well burned down, TR acted as chef, the fare usually consisting of chickens or steaks done in bacon fat. My own recollection is that he fried the meat in a good deal of fat, but Archie, who after fifty years of trial and error has become a good roaster, insists that his father, in fact *boiled* the steaks in grease. Whatever TR did with the food, we ate it greedily, sure that there was no better cook anywhere. Unless we had made a late start the favorite accompaniments were potatoes baked in the coals and lots of bread and butter, usually with a generous admixture of sand.

With dusk came a main part of the ritual—his telling us ghost stories, of which he remembered many. Usually someone called for a particular oft-told tale, to which the older boys listened as carefully as did the younger ones. Each of his four sons was quick to call TR's attention to any departure from his usual recital—a correction that he took with his ever-present good humor. I can see that these camping trips must have given him relief from the gruelling demands and restrictions of the presidency. Neither Archie nor I remember any secret service men or guards, even at a distance, when we camped on Lloyd's Neck.

No wonder that as children we adored this warm-hearted companion. The marvel is that with all the burdens of his official duties he not only made time to play with his children and their young cousins ("When I am at home," he wrote his friend Bob Ferguson, "I romp with the children about all the time I am not with Edith, riding, driving or rowing,")[3] but that he got so much fun out of his own relations with the youngsters, including even taking telephone messages for them. His daughter, Ethel Derby, remembers hearing the telephone ring at Sagamore as they were going in to breakfast—this was while he was still President—and his picking up the receiver and then grinning with delight.

When he hung up, he reported the following conversation:

SMALL BOY: "Is that you, Archie?"

TR: "No. This is Archie's father."

SMALL BOY: "Oh, well, you'll *do*. Tell Archie to be sure to come to supper tonight. Now, don't forget," and the small boy hung up. Whereupon TR quoted from Lewis Carroll: "How the creatures *do* order one about!"

3

DEVOTED PARTNER

Mrs. Theodore Roosevelt (Edith) stands out in my memory as a great and gracious lady, self-possessed but not egotistical, with a warm heart under a cool exterior. She personified order, duty, and discipline. We shunned her disapproval because we sensed that it was never expressed unless merited. I have known no one more completely in command of herself. If she felt fear she put it behind her. If ever she flinched she never showed it. Only once did I see her upset, and then only for a moment. This was just after word had come of her son Quentin's death in the Air Force. I had gone to Sagamore to say goodbye before sailing overseas with the 81st Division. When she saw me in uniform her eyes filled with tears and she turned away. Then she put her hand on my arm and said: "I'm all right, Nick; I'm all right." And she was.

The devotion between Theodore Roosevelt and Edith Carow dated from their childhood, when Edith had been a close friend of Theodore's sister Corinne and as children they had played together. Edith's grandfather, Isaac Carow, who was born on the island of St. Croix in the West Indies, had moved to New York in the early 1800s and was so successful in business that he was chosen president of the New York Chamber of Commerce and a director of the New York Hospital. His son

Charles, Edith's father, married Gertrude Elizabeth Tyler, whose family was connected with the Edwards and Pierponts. A cousin, Miss Edna Tyler, told me that Charles Carow had been in business with his father-in-law Tyler and that in his later years he suffered a breakdown and lost much of his fortune. But his daughter Edith had received an excellent schooling. She was an avid reader, loved music, was appreciative of the arts, and spoke and read French fluently.

My mother and my old friend Mrs. James Russell Parsons (like Edith, a childhood playmate of Corinne) told me that the friends of Theodore and Edith in the days of their youth took for granted that these two would marry. Doubtless there was surprise among them, therefore, when early in 1880 the engagement of Theodore to Alice Lee of Chestnut Hill, Massachusetts, was announced. The wedding was on his twenty-second birthday, October 27, 1880. Among the ushers were my father and his cousin Emlen Roosevelt and a number of Theodore's classmates. It is not without significance that two of the very few New Yorkers not related to the family who were invited by the Lees to stay with them for the occasion were Edith Carow and Fanny Smith (later Mrs. Parsons). Thus on this great occasion in Theodore's career that took him (supposedly forever) out of her own life, Edith was present. The suggestion that she be invited could only have come from him or had his approval.

Although I never knew Alice Lee I heard much about her. In my college years at Harvard I often made the trip from Cambridge to Chestnut Hill as TR had done thirty years previously, and, like him, I stayed with TR's classmate and friend Richard M. Saltonstall, whose son, Leverett, was a schoolmate and classmate of mine. As the Saltonstalls were cousins of the Lees I came to know three of Alice Lee's sisters—Mrs. Mumford (usually spoken of by her friends as "Bella"), Mrs. Grey (the "Rosie Lee" who figures prominently in the accounts of TR's days there), and Mrs. Fessenden. I can still see Mrs. Mumford, who must have been approaching her sixties, as the most popular person at "coming out" balls in Boston, sought after by a host of Harvard undergraduates with whom she danced with obvious delight, always full of fun and laughter and enjoying her popularity as if she were a debutante. These Lee sisters were typical of Boston's best—handsome, well educated, warmhearted and distinguished, with generations of good breeding behind them. If, as I am sure was the case, Alice Lee resembled them, I can well understand that she must have been a person of great charm and intelligence.

The tributes paid to Alice Lee when she died were obviously in recognition of her own fine qualities as well as in honor of her husband. Not only did the New York State Assembly, of which he was at the time a member, adjourn out of respect to her, but several members of the assembly spoke with warmth about her on the assembly floor—something rarely done in that legislative body about the deceased wife of a member. Her early death was almost more than TR could face. But it was characteristic of him that he went back to Albany three days after the funeral to take up his work in the assembly.

Alice Lee died in February, 1884. In October, 1886, Theodore became engaged to Edith Carow. The announcement was a surprise even to those who before his engagement to Alice Lee had expected that Theodore would marry Edith. Mrs. Parsons, referring to a letter from Theodore informing her that he was sailing to Europe to marry Edith, wrote: "Although during the previous winter I had seen both Theodore and Edith many times, I had not the slightest suspicion of this *dénouement*." My father was equally surprised, as may be judged from a letter that Edith gave me written by him to TR just after TR had told him of the engagement. Apparently fearing that his reaction might have given Theodore the impression that he disapproved, my father wrote:

> I am really more than pleased. I had hoped that you would marry, and had talked of the possibility of it with Laura [my mother—NR] who shares my view. Now that you are to marry a girl who has been one of my best friends, a girl whose main characteristic is truth, I am very much delighted.
>
> I know that you will be happy, and your happiness is much to me. I know that you will be a better man because you will have a fuller life. You are marrying a woman who can enter into your plans and who can appreciate your aims, and you have the best earnest of real happiness in that. You are marrying one who will love you—that is best of all.

That Edith appreciated Theodore's aims, entered into his plans, and loved him, is clear to all who knew this devoted couple as did we who, as youngsters, saw so much of them under so many different circumstances. It is noteworthy that James Amos, who for years served them as butler, wrote that he had never heard either of them say an impatient word to the other. Neither did I, nor did Ethel or Archie. Rarely were two such strong characters so happily married.

Edith's was not an easy life, even though it was rich and full. Ungregarious, she was married to a man who loved people and liked to be the center of attention. Where she was reserved he overflowed with exuberance and enthusiasm. Having early acquired the wisdom of maturity (a niece suggested that Edith had, in fact, been "born mature") she yet was wife to a man who kept much of the boy in him to the end. "Your cousin Edith," he once said to my sister, "sometimes thinks that I am the oldest and worst of her children!"—a remark that is more illuminating than he probably realized. Shrewd in her appraisal of people, she often saw men whom she distrusted imposing on her husband's good nature and kindness. Having lived through her father's loss of fortune, she found that she was financially dependent on a man who had little knowledge of, or interest in, household expenses. Practical by nature, she was more aware than was he of the insecurity and lack of continuity in the public life that so fascinated him. She knew that their increasing family and his own dwindling resources pointed to the need for him to earn a steady living—a need of which he was, of course, conscious, but which, with his capacity to take the overoptimistic point of view, he was inclined to put out of his mind. That he had the elements of greatness in him and might go far politically must have been clear to her. She understood him completely, knowing that she could not change him, but hoping that she might save him from himself and help him toward his goals.

Still further to complicate life for her was the fact that when she returned from her wedding trip to live in the house that Theodore had designed with and for his first wife she was faced with the problem of bringing up the child of that marriage. Not without reason the role of stepmother and stepchild has been considered difficult. In this particular collision of personalities it would be surprising indeed if Alice (later Mrs. Longworth), who in her youth showed the same spirit of fierce independence that she was to show throughout her life, had not sometimes earned her stepmother's disapproval—a disapproval that was neither selfish nor personal, but stemmed from deep-seated convictions of right and wrong. Devoted as I was to Alice's stepmother, I am sure that she could be stern when crossed—which must have been all the more difficult to bear because she so clearly personified principles of conduct that even youngsters sensed were hard to question. To a brilliant stepdaughter who at the turn of the century was imbued with the same kind of revolt against parental authority that has been widespread among teen-agers of the last half-century, the cold and detached insistence on standards of conduct by the wife of her adored father must have been trying—all the more so in that Edith Carow had a gift of seeing through people, old or young. The mere fact—and I have seen enough reliable evidence to accept it as a *fact*—that no one close to Alice with the exception of her Auntie Bye (TR's sister, Bamie) ever mentioned Alice's mother to her may well have subtly warped the development of this brilliant but basically unhappy person. It has been hinted that the initiative in this silence did not come from TR. This I find hard to accept because, had it been suggested to him that he keep silent, his fairness and kindness would have shown him the dangers and injustice to Alice in such a course. The only rational explanation that I have heard is that his determination to regard his first marriage and his life with Alice Lee as a chapter never to be reread was so great that he deliberately buried it in the recesses of his memory forever. In this connection it is not amiss to note that in his *Autobiography*, published in 1913, there is no reference whatever to Alice Lee —an omission that seems to me to belong on the debit side in any evaluation of his character.

Edith was a descendant of the stern and dominant New England revivalist preacher, Jonathan Edwards, and even though five generations removed from that redoubtable divine it is probable that she derived some of her strength from him and perhaps some of her deep sense of right and wrong, and her concept of duty. I am sure that neither of these formidable personalities was tolerant toward sinners. Certainly Edith was relentless in her disapproval of transgressors of the established code of morals and conduct. But her reaction was as detached as it was impersonal. She had been brought up in the conviction that there were things that simply were "not done." Had she herself sinned, she would have been the first to admit it and repent. The Episcopal Church, of which she was a member, was a constant source of strength to her, and she accepted unquestioningly its code of conduct. In the little church at Oyster Bay my mother's pew was directly in front of that of the Theodore Roosevelts. I can still hear the fervency in Edith's voice as, during the litany, she intoned the response: "Lord, have mercy upon us, and incline our hearts to keep this law." To her this was a reaffirmation of a way of life—something to cling to in good times and bad.

She fulfilled the social responsibilities imposed on her by her husband's official positions so long as she had the strength to do so. Inevitably she had to serve as hostess at countless meals and other gatherings and, like all official hostesses, she must have found the relentlessness of this sort of hospitality often not only boring, but physically exhausting. By instinct a charming hostess, by experience skilled in making guests welcome, she drew people out and encouraged them to talk—and this despite the fact that some were overawed by her great reserve. Rarely did she express opinions to casual acquaintances. Never would she talk politics. This was not because she lacked interest, but because she knew that whatever she said might be seized upon as reflecting TR's views.

As hostess at the White House her dignity and distinction of appearance were matched by an appropriate combination of friendliness and formality. I doubt if any First Lady since Dolly Madison better filled that exacting role. Mrs. Parsons, describing a visit to the White House just after TR succeeded to the presidency, wrote that "Edith had adjusted herself to her sudden and new environment with quiet dignity. She was serene and happy." Mrs. Parsons then went on to characterize Edith's marriage as "a singularly happy one through the long years—perhaps never more perfect than at that time." It is interesting that a recent biographer of TR, Edward Wagenknecht, who had not known Edith, expressed the opinion obviously derived from extensive studies of sources, that "Roosevelt would not have been Roosevelt without Edith Carow. In intelligence and character she was her husband's equal. In tact and judgment she was his superior."

Too intelligent and cultivated to be attracted by the vacuous and pretentious "leaders" of New York society, she liked best small gatherings of old friends—the Cabot Lodges, the Grant

LaFarges, the Winthrop Chanlers, the Owen Wisters, the James R. Garfields, Gifford Pinchot, Miss Emily Tuckerman, Mrs. Cadwalader Jones, to name but a few. With her intimates she could be sprightly and pointed, with keen comments on books and people. Her close friends were few. In the summer she saw much of my mother and of their cousin Christine (Mrs. W. Emlen Roosevelt), the three of whom often read aloud to each other. Occasionally she and my mother, who had been friends since childhood, would discuss with mingled humor and exasperation (I have this on my mother's say-so) the tribulations of being married to a Roosevelt—problems that other Roosevelt wives have faced in other generations, owing to the fact that most Roosevelt husbands have been, like Theseus in *A Midsummer Night's Dream,* "over-full of self-affairs."

In the running of the household and the disciplining of the children, Roosevelt wives usually have had the main responsibility, effectively backed, as a rule, by their men. Theodore gladly yielded to Edith's leadership, and it was her good fortune and that of the children that she was ably abetted by "Mame" Ledwith, who had been Edith's own nurse as a child. Mame was a warmhearted Irishwoman, who loved children as passionately as did Edith and Theodore, and whom the children adored and respected. Her love was not merely outgiving. She knew the value of discipline, and she could be depended upon to exercise firm control in the absence of the parents. It must have been a stormy, hilarious nursery, as each of the children, beginning with Edith's stepdaughter Alice, developed the Roosevelt traits of being not only self-absorbed but highly independent. Fortunately both parents were amused by the idiosyncrasies and antics of the children and took for granted that there would be rivalry among them. In a letter that TR wrote on March 12, 1894, to his friend, Robert Munro Ferguson, he described delightedly a recent uprising in the nursery. Alice then was ten, (and, incidentally, had told family friends several times that she had definitely given up her intention of having twins immediately),

Ted (Theodore, Jr.) was seven, Kermit five, Ethel three and a half, and Archie only a few months old. Kermit at the time had water-on-the-knee and was wearing some sort of metal brace that, while making him uncomfortable, in no sense dimmed his combative ardor. Kermit and Ethel, their father wrote,

> wage furious war on each other. The other day Ethel took away his go-cart, whereupon he charged her like a small heavy dragoon, bowled her over, and trundled off the cart. Ethel, who possesses much determination, and the temper and physique of a miniature James Corbett made a rapid flank movement round by the piazza, and in turn charged him and upset him. They then had it out, and she bit him and he used the weapon with which art had provided him by standing on his head and thumping her with his steel leg; about which period of the engagement a fond parent appeared on the scene and punished both combatants impartially.[1]

Edith's influence in TR's political life has sometimes puzzled biographers. Their daughter, Ethel Derby, told me in 1964 that "we all knew that the person who had the long head in politics was Mother, and that Father depended on her advice and judgment time and again." Knowing TR's faith in Edith's judgment and the closeness between them, it seems to me natural that he should often have talked with her about problems of policy and politics. I am sure that if and when he did so her reactions would have been expressed with a degree of detachment that would have helped him clarify his own thinking. Hermann Hagedorn[2] noted that she read the abstracts of press comments prepared for him by his secretaries and called his attention to items in the press that she felt he should read. Mark Sullivan, who knew the Roosevelts well and was an able journalist and editor, is quoted as having said that when TR lacked the benefit of her judgment about a man he was inclined to make mistakes, and added: "Never when he had his wife's judgment did he go wrong or suffer disappointment."

4

WORSHIPFUL SISTERS

In the early 1880s TR and my father bought land on Cove Neck, across the harbor from Oyster Bay, adjoining the summer home of their first cousin and close friend W. Emlen Roosevelt. The gang of children to whom I have referred spent their summers in the houses that these first cousins built. Owing to clannishness inherited from Dutch forebears, Roosevelt relatives were frequent visitors. Among these, TR's sisters, "Bamie" (Mrs. William Sheffield Cowles) and Corinne (Mrs. Douglas Robinson), were special favorites. These two were absorbed in TR and his career throughout his life. Close relatives have assured me that even when they married each had a larger place in her heart for her brother Theodore than for her husband. They were sure that no sisters ever had such a remarkable brother—which had a measure of truth in it. But it may be added that few great men had two such remarkable sisters. Both had charm and keen minds and were extraordinarily well read. Their conversation was vivid and their sense of fun almost as great as their brother's. They loved people and people loved them, and they lived joyously.

Bamie, I am sure, exerted a greater influence on Theodore than did Corinne, if for no other reason than that she was nearly four years his senior and that her mother had left much of the care of the younger children in Bamie's competent hands.

When the family went to Europe, Bamie was largely responsible not only for watching over the children but for seeing that Theodore kept up his studies. When, in 1876, Theodore entered Harvard as a freshman, it was Bamie who furnished his rooms in Cambridge for him and introduced him to her Boston friends. When he and Alice Lee were married in 1880 Bamie made the household arrangements for their honeymoon at her mother's place in Oyster Bay. When Alice Lee died two days after the birth of Alice Roosevelt, it was Bamie who took over his house and the care of his child. During much of the next two years Bamie kept house for TR and, being a popular hostess, did what she could to make life more bearable for him after the bitter blow of his wife's death. His welfare and his future continued to be Bamie's major concern throughout his life.

As I look back on my contact with Bamie and check my own impressions with those of her contemporaries and of members of my own generation who knew her well, I visualize a dominant, powerful character, accustomed to responsibility, with a strong sense of duty and with more subtlety than either her brother Theodore or her sister Corinne. She was capable of compassion, but she had a capacity for caustic disapproval that the other two lacked. Mrs. Parsons, who was only five or six years younger than Bamie, always thought of her only as a grownup, and remembered in particular "a certain authoritative attitude which was never questioned."[1]—a contemporary reaction that I think is illuminating. The last time that I saw Mrs. Parsons, which was in the mid-forties, she mentioned a certain "ruthlessness" in Bamie, which she attributed to the fact that Bamie had so long minded other people's affairs that she found it easier to make her own decisions and keep her own counsel. If Bamie thought that someone should do something—or should not do it—she had her way, however arbitrary she may have seemed to the person she was directing. Without being able to cite chapter and verse, my guess, based on my knowledge of

Bamie's character, is that her decisions were for the most part sound.

Bamie was plagued with pain much of her life, which may have been the cause of a certain occasional tartness in her speech and asperity in her reactions. Family tradition has it that she had been dropped by a nurse when very young and had sustained injury to her spine. Not only did this cause continuing discomfort, but it left her somewhat deformed. In her last twenty or thirty years she had, in addition, what doctors then called rheumatism, and later arthritis, characterized by very painful swelling of the joints. An account of her in her last years in the process of being dressed shows that almost every part of the ordeal was agonizing, as was the periodic changing of the position of her feet when she was in her chair after she was dressed. As she could not move them by herself this was done by the old family butler, Hopkinson, while guests were temporarily ushered into an adjoining room. As he moved her feet she was heard to murmur in her agony: "Oh, Hopkinson! Hopkinson! Oh, Hopkinson!" But she allowed nothing to interfere with her enjoyment of her friends. Sociable by instinct, she had early learned to center her attention on her companion of the moment so completely that that individual was convinced that Bamie had never before met anyone so fascinating. As a result the people with whom she talked not only gave to her the best of themselves but were sure that they had never known such an entrancing talker. Like her brother she had read widely and combined a retentive memory with a keen mind and with shrewdness in judging character. Her son Sheffield and her niece Corinne Alsop Cole, who for the last years of Bamie's life saw more of her than did other members of my generation, told me that they did not think that Bamie had TR's photographic memory, but they agreed that she retained clearly the essentials of what she read or heard.

Bamie had long been a friend of her distant cousin, J. Roosevelt Roosevelt (known as "Rosy"), son of James Roosevelt and half-brother of FDR. When Rosy's wife died in London where he was Secretary of the American Legation, he asked Bamie to come to London to serve as his hostess and to help look after his daughter Helen, which she did. Bamie was nearly forty, unattached, well off, with many friends and a love of social activities. Even though in those days—whether in Victorian England or provincial New York—it was unusual for a spinster to keep house for a widower other than an in-law, no family tradition of raised eyebrows has survived.

Bamie made many friends in London. Her responsiveness to people and her skill in drawing them out, together with her graciousness and charm, fitted her ideally for such a diplomatic post. Furthermore she had an interest in social customs and etiquette and with her capacious memory quickly came to know the social sheep from the goats. From Rosy she learned much about who was who in England, and she soon came to be of great help not only to him, but to Mrs. Bayard, the wife of the American minister. It takes tact, persistence, patience, and a large capacity to suffer bores gladly to be an effective, successful, and popular diplomatic host or hostess, all of which qualities Bamie had, in addition to a well-trained and well-stocked mind. "She grasped everything immediately, and she knew what should be done, and what the English expected of the Ambassadress," Rosy's daughter Helen told Hermann Hagedorn years later.[2] Furthermore, possessing a high degree of intelligence as well as great interest in world affairs, she was able to learn much from having a front-row seat in the capital of what was then the center of a great empire and the most powerful nation in the world. Political and diplomatic policies in Britain at the end of the nineteenth century were still determined, developed, and implemented by a small group of men, most of whom were interrelated by ties of marriage and descent and had had a common schooling. Many of these men were Bamie's friends and were fascinated by her charm and wit, and for years after she left

London they corresponded with her and when in the United States made it a point to visit her. When TR became President he profited from her knowledge of British politics and of world affairs.

In contrast to Bamie's circle of friends in London, most of the socially fashionable Americans whom she enjoyed seeing both before and after her years abroad lacked the intimate contacts with American political life that her English friends had with political life in London. In fact, most socially prominent New Yorkers viewed American political life with disdain; and even her close friend Mrs. Whitelaw Reid, whose husband was owner of the *New York Tribune*, knew and cared more about London high society than about the ins and outs of American politics—which is another way of saying that Bamie's American friends did not provide her with opportunities for following current events in America equal to those which her English friends had given her for following world affairs.

The granitic stability in Bamie was lacking in her sister Corinne, but to make up for it Corinne had much of her brother Theodore's gaiety and joy in life. More volatile than he, she was also more mercurial. As her daughter, Corinne Alsop Cole, said to me: "She could be full of fun and laughter one moment, and in tears the next." I think of her as constantly outgiving, full of enthusiasm, good humor, and geniality, and yet with great sensitivity. More gregarious than either Theodore or Bamie, she was quick to see the best qualities of people—and sometimes invested them with attributes that they did not, in fact, possess. She loved company and was constantly either serving as hostess or lunching or dining with her many friends. She was always the center of attention not only because of her ebullience and sense of humor but because of her warm absorption in others. Meals at the Robinson household were loud with laughter and, as she was adept in drawing out people, often rich in good talk. She guided conversation with a skill that would have been admired in French salons of a century ago. If someone had a story or an adventure to relate, she saw to it that he had the floor, which under the competition of the conversational roars of the male Robinsons was sometimes hard to achieve. The best sidelight on these tumultuous Robinson gatherings was given me by Corinne's close friend Fanny Parsons, in connection with the first visit that she paid to the Robinsons with her second husband, to whom she was newly married. She told me that, as Mr. Parsons had never met them, she warned him as they were leaving for the Robinsons' house: "Now, don't forget! Talk as loudly as you possibly can and answer your own questions!"

So great was Corinne's love of people and so generous was her enthusiasm for her friends, that she was not always a wise judge of character. Her daughter Corinne told me that she (Corinne, Jr.) often felt older than her mother and more mature—that there was something occasionally a little unworldly and naïve about her mother's reactions to people. The story still is told that after hearing a one-time friend of hers panned for what in those days was genteelly phrased "living in sin"—which, apparently, this man had done notoriously on a wide scale—she interjected in his behalf: "But he was *always* so *very* kind to so *many* young girls!" and was then somewhat surprised at the ribald hilarity with which her remark was received.

After her brother's death she devoted much of her time to the perpetuation of his memory. She wrote a book in tribute to him entitled *My Brother, Theodore Roosevelt* which, while excessive in its adulation, remains an important source for future biographers and historians. She also gave many lectures throughout the country and took an active part in Republican Party politics. I believe I am right in saying that when she seconded the nomination of Leonard Wood for President at the Chicago convention in 1920 this was the first time that a woman had been given this important assignment by the Republican National Committee. It is interesting to note in passing that her daughter, Corinne

Alsop Cole, seconded the nomination of Alf Landon at the Republican convention in 1936 and that her grandniece, Edith Williams (granddaughter of TR) in 1960 seconded the nomination of Richard M. Nixon.

It was characteristic of Corinne that in the 1932 campaign, in which Hoover ran for reelection, she, although a prominent Republican, announced that she could not take an active part in the campaign because Mr. Hoover's opponent (FDR) was the husband of her favorite niece, Eleanor. Just before the inauguration of FDR, Corinne died. *The New York Times,* not much given to eulogies, commented editorially as follows, under date of February 19, 1933:

> A "personage" has passed from America in the going of Mrs. Douglas Robinson—a "personage" endowed with rare perfections. She will be remembered most widely as the sister of "My Brother," Theodore Roosevelt, but there were circles in which she was herself the dominant personality. In sharing her memories of her illustrious brother, the "great sharer," as she called him, with the people "whom he loved so well" she did a sisterly act as devoted as that of the heroine in the Greek play, yet without a tragic passage in it. Even at his going there was but the sounding of trumpets on the other side.
>
> She said, after he had gone, that she "must go softly all my days" but the radiant zest which was in her as well as in him whom nations had crowned with their bays, would not let her go softly, even in the months when she was shut away from the light [by cataracts of the eyes]. The years were never mute to her. She continued her generous ardors to the end of her days with loyalty so deep to her heroes and her friends that she could neither see their faults nor the virtues of their opponents. As she said in her "Flight" she was "kin to the uttermost air, yet the daughter of man."

That her devotion to her niece Eleanor was reciprocated may be judged from the fact that President-elect and Mrs. Franklin D. Roosevelt were among the chief mourners at Mrs. Robinson's funeral.

Curiosity has been expressed about how TR's dynamic sisters got along with his wife Edith. Traditionally the relationship of in-laws is complicated by the prejudices of powerful personalities. The intensity of the devotion of these three highly possessive women to TR suggests that there must have been occasions when they failed to see eye to eye. Summarizing her estimate of the relations between Bamie and Edith, Eleanor (the wife of FDR) said: "There was basic devotion, but there must have been friction. How could there have been anything else when two women cared as much about a man, and they had such different qualities?"[3]

Theodore's marriage to Edith Carow inevitably meant that Bamie would no longer have the care of Theodore, his house and his child—which she had enjoyed and carried out effectively. Furthermore, having known Edith since she was a baby and being an astute judge of character, Bamie must have realized from the beginning that Edith would run Theodore's household in her own way, regardless of how Bamie had run it.

Yet through the years the two remained fast friends—and this despite the fact that some of those close to Bamie felt that Edith was the only person of whom Bamie was a little afraid. Even if and when Edith found Bamie's possessiveness irksome, I cannot believe that she failed to realize that it stemmed from Bamie's deep love of Theodore. Furthermore, Edith knew that both Bamie and Corinne could be—and were—helpful to Theodore in many ways and that they often had ideas about people and events that, even though they might differ from hers, helped him clarify his thinking. I believe that Eleanor (Mrs. FDR), who knew her Aunt Edith well and also had been First Lady, made a shrewd diagnosis when she said, with her own experience in the White House in mind: "A President has so little time and she [Mrs. TR] would feel I think sometimes that he enjoyed being with his sisters so much that it would take time which she wanted for herself and her children."[4] This, under the circumstances, seems in no sense a reflection on either Bamie or Corinne. Edith's time was limited, as was Theodore's. What more natural than that she wanted as much of his time for herself and her children as he could spare?

Theodore's daughter, Mrs. Richard Derby, gave me a sidelight on the relations between her mother and Bamie that seems to me significant. She told me that on the day of TR's funeral Mrs. Roosevelt asked Bamie if she might come up to Farmington to stay with her. Unless the relationship between these two strong personalities had been genuinely close, Edith would not have turned to Bamie at this particular moment in this particular way.

5

COSMOPOLITAN CONTACTS

THE BREADTH of TR's interests naturally brought him into contact with many men in different walks of life. Yet much as he enjoyed talking—and corresponding—with a host of people, he had relatively few intimates whom he saw repeatedly over a long period of years. Of his Roosevelt cousins among his contemporaries the two closest to him were my father, and their cousin Emlen. My father died at the age of thirty-seven, and Emlen remained a trusted adviser and close friend throughout TR's life. Of TR's Harvard associates those with whom he continued to keep in close touch were Henry Cabot Lodge, author and politician; Sturgis Bigelow, doctor of medicine and student of Buddhism; Winthrop Chanler, witty and gifted dilettante; Charles G. Washburn, member of Congress; Owen Wister, author of *The Virginian* and other novels and stories; William Roscoe Thayer, historian and biographer; and Robert Bacon, banker and subsequently Ambassador to France. Among others whom he saw often through the years were Grant LaFarge and his wife (LaFarge was a noted architect and son of the artist John LaFarge), and Dr. Alexander Lambert.

Throughout his life TR corresponded with, and often saw, numerous historians, including James Ford Rhodes, Sir George Otto Trevelyan, Archibald Cary Coolidge, Alfred Thayer Mahan, and Henry and Brooks Adams. Among diplomats, he saw much of "Springy" (Sir Cecil Spring-Rice, who had been best man at TR's wedding to Edith Carow and who later was Ambassador to the United States from Great Britain); Lord Bryce, author of *The American Commonwealth*, and also British Ambassador in Washington; Baron Speck von Sternburg, German Ambassador to the United States; Jules Jusserand, French Ambassador to the United States; and Henry White, who was one of the ablest American foreign service officers in a time when most American representatives abroad, of whatever rank, were intellectually innocuous heirs of large American fortunes.

Among the members of his cabinet who were particularly close to him were, of course, John Hay and Elihu Root, both of whom served him as Secretary of State; Charles J. Bonaparte, who was Secretary of the Navy and later Attorney General; William H. Moody, who also had been Secretary of the Navy, and whom TR subsequently appointed to the Supreme Court; James R. Garfield, Secretary of the Interior; and, although not actually of cabinet rank, Gifford Pinchot, who was his principal aide and guide in everything pertaining to conservation.

Because he was so keenly aware of the influence of the press TR maintained close relations with Washington correspondents and used many of these men in sounding out public reaction to actual or suggested policies. Among those close to him were Mark Sullivan, William Allen White, John J. ("Jack") Leary, O. K. Davis, Charles Willis Thompson, and William Hard. Almost without exception newspapermen assigned to cover him became and remained hero-worshipers—and this despite the fact that the newspapers that they represented were often antagonistic to TR. This was, of course, before the days of presidential press conferences.

As I look back over these people, many of whom I knew either in my youth or in my own career, I am inclined to think that those who had the greatest influence on TR were Henry Cabot Lodge, followed by Elihu Root, Gifford Pinchot, Admiral Mahan, Ambassador Jusserand, William Allen White, and W. Emlen Roosevelt.

I never knew Senator Lodge well, but heard and read much about him. There seemed to be something prickly about him—perhaps owing to shyness, or perhaps to mere mannerisms. He neither inspired friendship nor gave it freely. Rarely did he support a cause that might cost him votes, but when he gave his support it carried weight, especially with the conservative leaders of the Republican Party. He had the professional politician's respect for the party organization and reverence for party regularity, and yet he had an aristocrat's indifference to the impression that he made on people. He could be supercilious with ease—and often with intent—and in the main seemed to have little interest in his fellows. From my own few contacts with him I retain a clear picture of a highly intelligent, cultivated gentleman, rather small in stature, gracious to his friends, but self-centered, narrow, and unyielding. His continuing help and disinterested advice to TR from the days of the Republican National Convention in Chicago in 1884 onward stand out strikingly on the credit side of this constricted and purely practical partisan. It is no exaggeration to say that Lodge played a determining part in TR's career, not only as political adviser, but as effective wire-puller, contact man, supporter, and friend. Lodge, of course, found his intimacy with TR valuable during the latter's presidency. It added to his own prestige and influence. But it would be preposterous to say that this was why Lodge backed him as a young man. As early as 1885, a year after their collaboration in the fight against the nomination of Blaine as President, when TR was only twenty-seven years old, Lodge wrote in his journal: "Theodore is one of the most lovable souls as well as one of the cleverest and most daring men I have ever known"; and again: "The more I see him, as the fellow says in the play, 'the more and more I love him!' "[1] I find it easier to visualize TR's gratitude to Lodge than to think in terms of Lodge's devotion to TR.

But whatever may be said in criticism of Lodge no one can question the completeness of his loyalty to and affection for TR. Of course the two men differed from time to time. Lodge was distressed by TR's candidacy in the 1912 campaign. But each man respected and was devoted to the other. The friendship, while interrupted by the 1912 campaign, was not broken, and shortly after election day the split was forgiven and forgotten.

Elihu Root was a man of bigger stature than Lodge—certainly one of the outstanding Americans of the last hundred years. In a letter from TR to Andrew Carnegie dated February 18, 1910, TR said of him:

> Root was the man of my cabinet on whom I most relied, to whom I owed most, the greatest Secretary of State we have ever had, as great a cabinet officer as we have ever had, save Alexander Hamilton alone. He is as sane and cool-headed as he is high-minded; he neither lets facts blind him to ideals, nor ideals to facts; he is the wisest and safest of advisers, and staunchly loyal alike to friend and causes—and all I say I mean, and it is said with full remembrance that on certain points he and I would hardly agree.[2]

He was a wise counselor, an able advocate, relentless and efficient in defending the interests of his client—whether the client was the President of the United States when he, Root, was Secretary of State or was the Republican Party when he was chairman of the Republican National Convention in 1912 or some great corporation which, when he left political life, his law firm represented. I remember hearing TR praise this quality of Root's in the midst of the 1912 campaign, even though he (TR) believed that Root's defense of the Republican National Committee in Chicago, whose interests he as chairman of the convention felt bound to champion, had been shameless and dishonest.

In the early twenties I had several talks with Mr. Root, and when I was elected a member of the Century Club he was still its president. All who had known him held him in highest esteem, both professionally and personally. It is interesting to reread TR's comparison between Root's services as Secretary of State and those of his predecessor, John Hay. Jack Leary, in his *Talks with TR,* quotes TR as saying: "It is because Root would not hesitate to express an opinion that he was immensely more valuable to me in the cabinet than John Hay was. Hay was a splendid character, likeable and lovable, but he would never citicize. He wouldn't fight for an opinion. Root would, and he'd give persistent battle for his viewpoint. He was a most dogged fighter." Leary went on to tell how TR, when he sent a state paper to Root for editing, often found that he could hardly recognize the document when Root sent it back, and Leary added that TR remarked: "Sometimes I was very thankful I could not."

Root's own description of Hay, made in a memorial address, was that Hay was "unassuming, retiring, self-effacing." Root stressed Hay's refinement, sensitiveness, and reserve and spoke highly of his sense of humor, which he described as "exquisite, delicate and subtle." Hay's estimate of men and their lives, Root continued, "cut through all appearances to the realities, were independent of clothes and houses and the accidents of manners, and seized upon whatever was true and human, whether it was in the miner's hut, or the farmer's ranch or the millionaire's palace. The scope of his human sympathy was universal. He had a fine sense of proportion, of the fitness of things."[3]

It is interesting, in the light of this background, to read Hay's account of TR as President. It centers on an after-dinner conference at the White House composed of TR, Secretary Hay, and Mr. Root, who at that time was Secretary of War. After the three men had discussed a crisis in Santo Domingo, the President, said Hay:

sent for his stenographer and dictated a brief message he proposes to send to the Senate next week. It was a curious sight. I have often seen it and it never ceases to surprise me. He storms up and down the room dictating in a loud and oratorical tone, often stopping, recasting a sentence, striking out and filling in, hospitable to every suggestion, not in the least disturbed by interruptions, holding on stoutly to his purpose, and producing finally out of these most unpromising conditions a clear and logical statement which he could not improve with solitude and leisure at his command.[4]

In his memorial address on John Hay, Mr. Root recalled that Hay, while he was private secretary of Abraham Lincoln, lived most of the time in the White House. At numerous cabinet meetings Hay referred to these years and told how Mr. Lincoln slept in a room at the western end of the White House and he, Hay, slept in a little room at the southeastern corner. The picture that Root gave as he got it from Hay follows:

The President [Lincoln] oppressed and disturbed by the cares and perplexities and nervous tension of the great war, was often sleepless, and often, when he had long sought sleep in vain, he would rise and go down to the boy's room and waken him in the dead of night, and sitting on the edge of his bed would read aloud to him from some favorite book until the current of thought was changed and sleep seemed possible. Sometimes it was the Bible; sometimes Shakespeare; sometimes Tom Hood. The spiritual insight of the great liberator divined in the soul of the boy the sympathy and responsiveness which returned to the reader a calm and solace he could not find in the cold dull page alone. How often have the listeners to that tale, as their duties brought them again and again to the scene, imagined the tall, gaunt form of Lincoln clad in white, passing down the long dimly lighted corridor, seeking comfort against his cares from the sympathy of the noble youth in the thoughts to which he loved to turn. Was ever a boy so fortunate! Was ever a character so influenced and guided in the development of its most impressionable years. From that time, we may well believe, came Hay's large and kindly view, the deep sense of the seriousness of life, the wit and humor and sensitiveness to impressions of the beautiful, the genuine love of his country and its people, the love of humanity, of peace and justice with mercy, the capacity for loyalty to great causes, the unquestioning realization of duty to play a man's part in the world of action.[5]

Gifford Pinchot was described in TR's autobiography as "the man to whom the nation owes most for what has been accomplished as regards the preservation of the natural resources of our country." After detailing specific actions of Pinchot, TR concluded by saying that "among the many, many public officials who under my administration rendered literally invaluable service to the people of the United States, he, on the whole, stood first." The association of the two men had begun when TR was governor of New York. It ripened into a close friendship based on mutual interests, mutual respect, and a clear-headed realization that Pinchot's knowledge of the over-all problem of conservation was of immense value to TR and that with TR's active support he, Pinchot, could accomplish much for the cause that throughout his life was dearest to him.

In my youth Mr. Pinchot was a favorite of the youngsters. After TR's death I saw him from time to time, and continued my affection and respect for him. He was a man of singular charm, physically rugged but spiritually sensitive, a born crusader, with no personal interests at stake. A passionate advocate of conservation, he not only inspired many others to take up the cause, but was a shrewd campaigner in its behalf. It is no exaggeration to say that all who in the last half century have battled in behalf of the preservation of our natural resources would have been completely helpless had it not been for Pinchot's pioneering and for his vision. As we shall see in a later chapter, the campaign met with constant defeats. But had it not been for Pinchot, working through TR, there would be little left today anywhere in the United States of the nation's scenic resources.

How good Pinchot was as a political adviser is more difficult to assess. But TR had so many sources of political opinion and advice that he did not depend on Pinchot in politics so much as in conservation. Mr. Pinchot has been charged with having "poisoned" TR's mind about the Taft administration because he (Pinchot) met TR in Europe on his way home from his African safari and briefed him about what had happened in Washington since March 4, 1909, when Taft became President. If TR began to have misgivings about Taft the reason would surely stem from what the new President had—or had not—done, not from any "slant" that Mr. Pinchot might have given the former President in his "briefing."

The influence of Admiral Mahan on TR seems to me to have been greater than TR's biographers have recognized. Mahan's writings clarified the true role of sea power in international affairs and helped TR to understand more clearly the over-all relationship of the great world powers, as well as the particular interests of the United States in world affairs. Mahan's published analyses of the growing tension between Germany and Great Britain aroused great interest in England and were available to thoughtful Americans who were uneasy about the obviously increasing imminence of the war, which finally started in August, 1914. From the days of TR's service as Assistant Secretary of the Navy down through the presidency and the outbreak of World War I, he consulted Mahan freely and showed a continuing interest in all of Mahan's writings.

The friendship between President Roosevelt and the French Ambassador, Jules Jusserand, was close because of M. Jusserand's literary background and because of the fact that his candor was unimpeachable. Most diplomats make a profession of being noncommittal. The French language, as the then accepted language of diplomacy, was used, among other reasons, because of its subtlety and ambiguity. M. Jusserand was a master of English as well as of French, and doubtless, had he been so inclined, he could have been charmingly and plausibly evasive in both. But TR, in a letter that he wrote to Jusserand in 1906, paid tribute to what he termed the two dominant notes in the ambassador's personality—his unfailing soundness of judgment and his high integrity of personal conduct. The relationship between the two men was, as TR said, one that "has very, very rarely obtained between any Ambassador at any time and the head of the government to which that Ambassador was accredited." Throughout the remainder of his life TR knew that he could trust Jusserand to speak honestly and frankly. This knowledge in itself was a great help to TR in understanding the rapidly changing power struggle in Europe.

William Allen White is now all but forgotten in the United States. But for the half-century beginning in 1890 he was a successful small-town editor who, although an apostle of political reform, was at heart a conservative. White was an engagingly shrewd spokesman for all that was best in the rural America of the previous generation, and an inlander who looked on the Atlantic and Pacific oceans as "moats defensive" against hostile foreigners. He first met TR when the latter had become Assistant Secretary of the Navy, and, according to his autobiography, White "was afire with the splendor of the personality" that he had met. "He poured into my heart," White explained, "such visions, such ideals, such hopes, such a new attitude toward life and patriotism and the meaning of things, as I had never dreamed men had."[6] That the reaction was by no means one-sided may be judged from the fact that in a long letter to White dated February 6, 1900, while TR was still governor of New York, he wrote: "you are among the men whose good opinion I crave and desire to earn by my actions. I rank you with, for instance, Judge Taft of Cincinnati and Jim Garfield of Cleveland."[7] White in time became a Bull Mooser and had countless useful contacts among politicians and editors throughout the Midwest. In my newspaper years I saw him often, and lunched with him occasionally at the Century Club, of which we both became members at about the same time. I always found him an engaging, intelligent, and interesting talker, whose judgment on opinion in the Midwest was likely to be sound and enlightening.

I have listed Emlen Roosevelt because, of them all (including even Lodge) he had been closest to TR since childhood. His devotion and admiration for TR was great, and as he was himself of unimpeachable integrity and knew well the leading figures in the business world, he was in a position to give TR information and advice that TR could evaluate through his own intimate knowledge of Emlen's personal rectitude. To the members of my generation Emlen seemed a rather austere person. But we sensed his integrity and enjoyed his dry humor. He was a banker of the old school—conservative and cautious—who had inherited his father's private banking firm of Roosevelt and Son and by a combination of prudence and shrewdness had made a substantial fortune. TR valued his opinions on financial and economic matters, which the two often discussed in our presence.

The organization of the Progressive Party in the 1912 campaign brought new friends to TR at the same time that it alienated old ones. Among the most active supporters of the Bull Moose campaign were George W. Perkins and Elon Huntington Hooker. TR had known both men when he was governor of New York, and had appointed Perkins a member of the New York Interstate Palisade Park Commission. Both men gave devoted service—and substantial contributions—to the Progressive cause. Perkins, as a partner of J. P. Morgan, had aroused distrust among many of the Bull Moosers from the Midwest, who had perpetuated the tradition that New York bankers in general, and Morgan partners in particular were in league with the devil. The score was partly balanced by the fact that many of the most ardent Bull Moosers of the West were looked upon by TR's New York followers as wild-eyed and dangerous radicals. Only the magnetism of TR's exuberant personality held together persons of so many widely divergent views—and this only for the duration of the campaign. But while dissension was unavoidable, most of the Bull Moosers kept their loyalty and devotion to TR, even after his decision in 1916 to refuse the nomination of the Progressive Party for the presidency.

It was among his conservative friends that bitterness against him ran deepest. Henry Adams, whom Owen Wister listed as among TR's intimates, wrote to his brother Brooks as early as February, 1912, that TR's "mind has gone to pieces and has disintegrated like the mind of society, until it has become quite incoherent and spasmodic. He is, as Taft justly said, a neurotic, and his neurosis may end like LaFollette's, in nervous collapse or a stroke or acute mania."[8] While many of Adams' friends and associates doubtless agreed with him, Adams' antipathy toward TR was nothing new. In leafing over Adams' published letters I found numerous references to Adams' annoyance with TR's tendency to monopolize the conversation. Writing to his close friend, Mrs. Don Cameron, on January 12, 1902, he observed: "As usual, Theodore absorbed the conversation. If it tried me ten years ago it crushes me now."[9] A little later in this same letter Adams says: "Really, Theodore is exasperating, even to me, and always was. . . . What annoys me is his childlike and infantile superficiality, with his boyish dogmatism of assertion. He lectures me on history as though he was a high school pedagogue." Two years later Adams wrote the same correspondent about another dinner at the White House: "We were overwhelmed in a torrent of oratory, and at last I heard only the repetition of I, I, I, attached to indiscretions greater one than another."[10]

I met Adams only once. This was after I returned from the Embassy in Paris in 1916. Mrs. Cameron, whom I had often seen in Paris, had written to him suggesting that I call on him. He invited me to dine with him alone. I remember vividly the small, fragile, bearded figure, pale and gray, seated at a table lighted only by candles, kindly receiving the youngster of twenty-three and full of questions about Paris in World War I. His courtesy was obviously out of deference to Mrs. Cameron. I have no notes of our talk, and I doubt if TR's name was even mentioned. But from all that I heard and read about him—I had known several of Mrs. Adams' own nieces and of his adopted "nieces"—I find it hard to visualize close friendship between men so different in character as Henry Adams and Theodore Roosevelt. That they saw much of each other I do not doubt. The Theodore Roosevelts, like the Cabot Lodges, had been frequent guests of the ever-hospitable Adams. But mere frequency of social contact does not, by itself, necessarily mean close friendship. Adams was a pessimist, a theorist, a passivist. TR was an ebullient doer. Adams took a grim pleasure in all that was worst in American and world affairs, and looked on the contemporary American political scene with disdain. TR was not only an optimist, but by instinct a reformer and, being a practical man engaged in public life, he used the existing machinery of politics in the pursuit of reforms that he deemed necessary. To Adams this was a blemish, as may be judged from the fact that he wrote to his English friend Charles Milnes Gaskell that "my neighbor Roosevelt is a terrible bore owing to his absorption in cheap politics."[11]

While there is only one downgrading reference to Adams by name in the eight volumes of TR's published correspondence, there are attacks on the novel, *Democracy*, whose authorship by Adams in the early eighties was long concealed. As late as 1905 TR, commenting on it, said: "It was written by Godkin, perhaps with assistance from Mrs. Henry Adams. It had a superficial and rotten cleverness, but it was essentially false, essentially mean and base, and it is amusing to read it now and see how completely events have given it the lie."[12] In a letter to Owen Wister in April, 1906, TR referred again to the book, saying: "I think poorly of the author of *Democracy*, whoever he or she may have been."[13] To George Horace Lorimer of the *Saturday Evening Post* he characterized *Democracy* as a "bright, sinister little novel" that reflected the opinions of "what the cultivated cynics of that period thought of public men and public opinion then."[14]

Both Adams and TR had a large measure of egocentricity. Adams, surrounded by devoted listeners and admirers, and expecting to be the center of social gatherings, obviously found

TR's conversational exuberance intolerable. It would not be surprising if TR had been irked by Adams' preoccupation with the degradation of the democratic dogma. But the company at Adams'—as at the White House during TR's presidency—was almost sure to be interesting and the conversation of either monologist stimulating.

6

INSATIABLE CURIOSITY

TR HAD ONE of the most effective minds of any of the men with whom, as journalist or diplomat, I came in contact—men such as Winston Churchill, Herbert Hoover, Georges Clemenceau, Henry Adams, Elihu Root, John Dewey, FDR, Henry L. Stimson, Mussolini—to list but a few. His intellect was in no sense creative or even speculative. He lacked the illuminating wit and old-world cynicism of Clemenceau. Unlike Churchill he neither spoke nor wrote with exceptional clarity and force. But he had a breadth and thoroughness of background based on extensive and intensive reading in many fields, buttressed by a phenomenal memory. Thanks to his quickness in perceiving and soundness in evaluating essentials he was a shrewd analyst. In political matters he was skilled in distinguishing between the desirable and the possible. James Bryce, author of *The American Commonwealth,* who had been close to TR for years, told Owen Wister that TR "had a brain that could always go straight to the pith of any matter," and added: "That is a mental power of the first rank."[1]

Broad as was his intellectual equipment he was not emotionally objective. His likes were as strong as his dislikes. Just as he stood by his friends staunchly he castigated his enemies unmercifully—and he was effective in his choice of dramatic epithets with which to ridicule opponents. Often those against whom he was prejudiced deserved his disapprobation, but there were, of course, striking exceptions—as witness his strong prejudice against Winston Churchill, who, when TR died in 1919, had shown little promise of his ultimate greatness, but who, as we later came to see, surpassed TR in mental equipment and equaled him in moral and physical courage. Owing in no small measure to the intensity of TR's emotional reactions, he made mistakes, but as he himself pointed out in a reply to a man who had upbraided him for having been mistaken: "For every mistake of mine of which you know I know of at least ten."

If his emotional reactions sometimes misled him, they yet often were politically valuable. His enthusiasms and prejudices, when dramatized by his gift for apt phrases and his histrionic skill, aroused keen response. So did his tendency to moralize, which brought on him the criticism that he had invented, or at least discovered, the Ten Commandments. As his close friend, Owen Wister, emphasized, he had much of the "preacher militant" in him. In the course of his upbringing he had been deeply impregnated with a sense of right and wrong, fairness and unfairness, justice and injustice, which had often led him to judge complex problems of policy in terms of moral values. While his concepts of what men should and should not do were necessarily somewhat restricted by the remnants of the caste tradition in England and the United States down into the middle of the nineteenth century, he was ahead of most of his contemporaries in fighting privilege and in insisting that integrity of conduct was to be expected as much from the rich and the politically powerful as it was from less fortunate people.

Doubtless this sort of reforming impetus was of great value in the drab era of industrial and corporate expansion in the post-Civil War decades. Perhaps it is an overgeneralization to say that those to whom during his presidency TR attached the label of "malefactors of great wealth" were lawless as well as shameless in their greed. No one, however, who reads the history of financial and industrial expansion beginning with Grant's administration and running down to the start of the First World War can fail to be struck with the extent to which even men of basically good character took for granted that the role of government was to foster the exploitation of the natural resources of the country by the shrewd—or unscrupulous—minority that had managed to acquire access to the nation's mines, forests, and waterways and that government should be of the rich, by the rich (or their tools), and for the rich.

It is hard to draw a line between TR's natural endowments and his deliberately cultivated attainments. As I look back with the benefit of fifty years of hindsight and much reading a number of points stand out about his mental equipment.

The first is, of course, the breadth of his knowledge. Few men have read so extensively and perceptively in as many such varied fields—zoology and ornithology, history and biography (both ancient and modern), poetry, and fiction (both early and modern), and contemporary reviews and magazines. As a boy he had been steeped in the King James Version of the Bible, and in *Pilgrim's Progress* and in *Paradise Lost* and knew many portions of these by heart. Latin he had also learned, but little or no Greek. He read German and French easily (but spoke them unidiomatically, and with a happy disregard for the rigors of grammar) and enough Italian to enjoy Dante in the original. His reading habits were literally insatiable and omniverous. In a letter to Sir George Otto Trevelyan, the English historian, written in 1906, he gave an illuminating sidelight on this:

> I find it a great comfort to like all kinds of books and to be able to get half an hour or an hour's complete rest and complete detachment from the fighting of the moment by plunging into the genius and misdeeds of Marlborough, or the wicked perversity of James II, or the brilliant battle for human freedom fought by Fox, or, in short, anything that Macaulay wrote or that you have written, or any one of the novels of Scott, and some of the novels of Thackeray and Dickens, or to turn to Hawthorne or Poe, or to Longfellow, who I think has been underestimated of late years, by the way.[2]

In another letter to Trevelyan written at the end of 1904 he said that during the presidential campaign of that year he reread Trevelyan's history of the American Revolution "and liked it more than ever, but came to the conclusion that you had painted us a little too favorably. I also re-read both your Macaulay and your Fox and then re-read Macaulay's history. . . . I read a number of other books during the campaign, Rhodes' excellent history, for instance, and a good deal of Dickens"[3]—all of this while carrying the full burden of the presidency and the time-consuming distractions of pulling potentially unfriendly politicians into line and making appropriate public addresses to strengthen his appeal to the electorate. Throughout his life he always had a book within easy reach, often reading short snatches between appointments and sometimes even reading while he was dressing. As his reference to Macaulay suggests, he reread as well as read. While never an ardent Shakespearean, he included Shakespeare's plays in his "Pigskin Library," which he took on his hunting expedition in Africa in 1909–10 and, in the course of a letter to Cabot Lodge, noted that he was reading and rereading them with the greatest satisfaction. I remember his telling me, as he was leaving Sagamore Hill for New York on the June morning in 1912 when he was awaiting word as to whether he should go to Chicago to be present at the Republican National Convention: "I am taking Ferrero and Herodotus with me to amuse myself and get my mind off the business if I go to Chicago."[4] He had read Ferrero's volumes on ancient Rome on numerous occasions and, of course, knew Herodotus thoroughly. To reread them under the stress of the political climax would be a welcome diversion and distraction.

Only his great powers of concentration and close attention made it possible for him to read as much and as fast as he did. Whether in a room with others or on a train or surrounded by noise and movement he could bury himself in a book. Friends and associates have testified that not only would he leaf through a volume at a speed of two or three pages a minute, but that he retained the substance, and in many cases the actual wording, of what he read. William Allen White, the Kansas editor, wrote in his autobiography about watching TR, during a campaign trip, rapidly leafing through J. Arthur Thomson's ponderous volume, *Heredity*. White interrupted TR with a facetious question about what he might be getting out of the book by turning the pages so quickly. Whereupon TR handed him the volume and asked White to examine him on the contents as far as he had read. "I did," White wrote in his autobiography.[5] "It was letter perfect. It was one of the most extraordinary mental feats I ever saw." On another occasion—this time while inspecting an Arabic library in Egypt in 1910—TR asked the interpreter, who was showing him an Arabic manuscript of the travels of Ibn Batuta, (an Arabian counterpart of Marco Polo), if he could find a particular passage, the substance of which TR quoted in English, giving the approximate location. To the interpreter's astonishment he found the Arabic text almost exactly as TR had quoted it in English. Lawrence Abbott, who was present, added by way of explanation that TR had read a French translation of the Arabic years previously and remembered it well enough to be able to identify its location.[6]

Abbott also told of an experience of Charles Patrick Neill, when U. S. Commissioner of Labor, taking to TR in the White House a report that represented much study. TR, as Abbott put it, turned over the typewritten sheets "about as steadily and rapidly as an old-fashioned grandfather's clock ticks, finished the document and handed it back to the Commissioner with comments and suggestions so fresh and pertinent that it was quite clear that he had not only read the words of the report but had clearly understood its scope and significance." Mr. Neill's comment was that it had taken TR less than thirty minutes to understand, and to improve by adding new facts and arguments, the treatment of a subject to which he (Neill) had devoted hours of study.[7]

Further testimony of the range of his capacious memory was given me by Hungary's "Grand Old Man," Count Albert Apponyi, whom I saw often when I was Minister to Hungary in the early 1930s. He had met TR not only in the White House but during TR's visit to Vienna in 1910 on returning from Africa to the United States. Apponyi marveled at TR's accurate knowledge of relatively small details of Hungary's history, some of them running back for centuries. On one of Apponyi's visits to the United States before World War I he told my mother that TR had quoted to him practically verbatim an account that he had read about an early Hungarian hero, and that when he, Count Apponyi, showed surprise that TR could quote so extensively and so accurately, the President said that he had read this item some twenty years previously and had not thought of it since.

It has sometimes been said of TR that like the English historian Thomas Babington Macaulay he had what is called a "photographic memory." Whether or not either man's recollection of what he read was actually complete, there can be little doubt that it was extraordinarily accurate and voluminous. In this connection I was interested to hear from TR's daughter, Ethel Derby, that Sir George Otto Trevelyan, who was a nephew of Macaulay and had known him well, told her in Rome in 1910 that TR was the only man he knew whose memory could be described as equal to that of Macaulay.

Prolific as was TR's reading it was also discriminating. He was quick to detect merit and to praise the good points of a new author—often before specialists admitted that the man deserved recognition. A typical example of his alertness to merit occurred in connection with the publication in the first week in May, 1890, by Little Brown and Company, of a book entitled *The Influence of Sea Power on History* by an American naval officer named Alfred Thayer Mahan. Within a few days of its release TR, at that time a member of the Civil Service Commission in Washington, wrote the author as follows: "During the last two days I have spent half my time, busy as I am, in reading your book. That I found it interesting is shown by the fact that, having taken it up, I have gone straight through and finished it. . . . It is a very good book—admirable; and I am greatly in error if it does not become a naval classic."[8] When an English edition was published a year later it was hailed by the *London Times* as a "really great book." Within three years of its publication Mahan was given honorary degrees in Oxford and Cambridge in recognition of the importance of the volume, and it was translated into German and other languages. The German Kaiser, William II, telegraphed his friend, Poultney Bigelow, describing Mahan's volume as "a first class book," and added: "It is on board all my ships and constantly quoted by all my captains and officers."[9] When Mahan died in 1914 the *London Morning Post* characterized him in an editorial as "the greatest among Naval historians." Certainly he did more than any other historian before his time to make plain the close interrelationship between naval and military strength on the one hand and the attainment of diplomatic objectives on the other. *The Influence of Sea Power on History* has become not only a naval classic but indispensable to students of international affairs.

Three years after the publication of this book a then relatively unknown American professor of history, Frederick Jackson Turner, delivered an address before the American Historical Association entitled "The Influence of the Frontier on American History." Within a few weeks of its publication he received a letter from Civil Service Commissioner Roosevelt, in which TR said, among other things: "I think you have struck some first class ideas, and have put into definite shape a good deal of the thought which has been floating around rather loosely."

The fact that TR had also written in the fields in which Mahan and Turner were writing naturally inclined him to read their books with special interest. But it is particularly significant that TR was among the first to recognize that the two works referred to were of exceptional merit and would be of far-reaching influence and to urge that they be widely read. I doubt if any other office-holder in the United States at the time (including the overwhelming majority of naval officers) had ever heard of Captain Mahan or of Frederick Jackson Turner or would have bothered to read what either wrote.

It was also characteristic that when Owen Wister discussed with TR the possibility of using Wister's published short stories of the range country as the substance of a novel, TR thought well of the suggestion but urged Wister not to include in the novel any reference to an instance of shocking brutality to a horse that formed the basis of one of Wister's stories entitled *Balaam and Pedro*. TR maintained that the incident would arouse so much resentment and disgust that it would affect adversely the reception of the proposed novel. Wister was unconvinced by TR, but as the development of the story into a novel was delayed, he postponed final decision about the advice. On consulting TR again later Wister reluctantly agreed to delete the offending incident, and the novel was published without it. This novel—*The Virginian*—became and long remained a best seller and was in fact the prototype of countless westerns.

TR's relations with Finley Peter Dunne shows a slightly different aspect of his reaction to writers. At the turn of the century Dunne's articles, which centered on an engaging Irishman called "Mr. Dooley" and might be described as being a form of literary cartoon, were widely syndicated and read. Apart from their humor they contained shrewd comments and criticisms on the contemporary scene—many of them making fun of TR. Ordinarily political leaders are sensitive to widely publicized criticism—and TR was not exempt from this tendency. But from his first readings of Dunne's comments he sensed that the author of "Mr. Dooley" had an independent and honest mind, as well as a good sense of humor. On reading "Mr. Dooley's" review of TR's book about the Rough Riders, published under the heading: "Alone in Cubia," TR wrote Dunne an enthusiastic letter, inviting him to lunch at Sagamore. The ensuing friendship endured through the years, despite the fact that "Mr. Dooley" was openly critical of many things that TR did.

Another of TR's enthusiasms was the poet Edward Arlington Robinson, whom he not only assisted financially, but also praised publicly—to the indignation of proprietary critics of American poetry who resented the intrusion of a mere politician into the field of poetical appraisal. He was among the early admirers of the novelist Edna Ferber and of the journalist Walter Lippmann, as well as Lippmann's mentor, Herbert Croly, editor of *The New Republic*. TR was eager for sound information and welcomed factual instruction as well as thoughtful advice—as may be seen from the fact that Elihu Root called TR "the most advisable man I ever knew"[10]—which is another way of attesting the man's receptivity and intellectual responsiveness.

TR's memory was not confined to what he read. He remembered people whom he had met merely casually—and a man in his position must, of course, have met literally thousands of persons. He could not remember most of these persons by name, but given a clue as to the place of the meeting he could frequently recall the occasion and make an appropriate remark. During the summer of 1913, which I spent in northern Arizona with him and his sons Archie and Quentin, we saw on numerous occasions someone approach him with the usual: "You don't remember me, Colonel, but I met you at ——" and then identify the place. TR would look at him for a few seconds and then say: "Yes, and you told me . . ." and then fill in some detail of what the man had said to him.

TR's early interest in ornithology and natural history may

well have helped to mold his memory. I believe that psychologists now postulate a direct connection between the process of remembering and the process of deliberately paying close attention. Ornithologists in particular find it essential to watch for very small variations in color and form of birds and find it helpful to be able to detect, classify, and recall these variations without having to refer to textbooks. From early youth TR was fascinated by birds and shot, stuffed, mounted, classified, and wrote about them. He studied the ornithology not only of various portions of the United States, but also of parts of Europe and the Near East, in both of which regions he spent months in his childhood. In spite of the fact that he could not "carry a tune" he learned the songs of countless birds and could even distinguish differences between subspecies by their songs. Sir Edward Grey, famous in England as foreign minister at the outbreak of World War I, who, like TR, was a bird lover, recorded that when he and TR went on a two-day bird walk in the New Forest in 1910, TR was able to identify English birds by their song when these were kin to American birds. "It is seldom," said Viscount Grey, "that you find so great a man of action who was also a man of such wide and accurate knowledge. I happened to be impressed by his knowledge of natural history and literature and to have had first-hand evidence of both, but I gather from others that there were other fields of knowledge in which he was also remarkable." And again: "I saw enough of him to know that to be with him was to be stimulated in the best sense of the word for the work of life."[11]

7

CAPTAIN OF HIS SOUL

THOSE WHO KNEW TR well believed him to be free from fear. As youngsters we had assumed that he was born that way, apparently reflecting his own belief that there are persons who are "naturally fearless"—(the phrase is his)—a belief that modern psychologists question. But in his autobiography he stated that he was not among the "naturally fearless," but had acquired fearlessness by deliberate practice, and he insisted that anyone who really wants to overcome fear can do so. In elaborating this idea he said that what he called "nerve control" and "cool-headedness" could be acquired by custom and repeated exercise of self-mastery. "This is largely a matter of habit in the sense of repeated exercise of will-power," he explained. "If the man has the right stuff in him his will grows stronger and stronger with each exercise of it—and if he has not the right stuff in him he had better keep clear of dangerous game hunting, or indeed of any other form of sport or work in which there is bodily peril."[1] He went on to say that having been a rather sickly and awkward boy he was, as a young man, at first both nervous and distrustful of his prowess. "I had to train myself painfully and laboriously, not merely as regards my body, but as regards my soul and spirit."[2] In later life he developed what he called his "philosophy of bodily vigor as a method of getting that vigor of soul without which vigor of body counts for nothing." That TR believed that these two types of vigor were—or could be made to be—interdependent seems clear, but many of us have known persons displaying vigor of soul who lacked bodily vigor, as well as strong men with weak souls. *Spirit, soul, will-power, nerve-control, coolheadedness, the right stuff*—these terms as he used them sound today more like a moralist's message than like contributions to clarification of metaphysical speculation.

Their pertinence lies in the fact that what he described as training his soul and spirit was at the very foundation of his success in life and helps explain what set him apart from—and above—his fellows. Not only did he banish fear, but by deliberate, conscious effort he attained an extraordinarily high degree of self-mastery, both physical and moral. In his autobiography he ascribed to a chance encounter with two older boys, against whose bullying he found himself physically helpless, his initial decision to transform his weak and almost sickly frame into a powerful, robust body. While this particular instance doubtless dramatized his condition—and its remedy—I am inclined to think that the real impetus to his intention to master himself derived from his long struggle against asthma throughout his boyhood. Fortunately for him, his father, whom he adored, encouraged him in his fight for health and strength, and this was for him, in the words of the psalmist, "a very present help in trouble." But in the final analysis it was he himself who shaped himself, not only physically, but spiritually. Throughout his life he was the captain of his soul. Just as he started early to build his body, so he early set—and lived up to—standards for himself that most persons would have found hard indeed to maintain—standards of conduct only realizable through stern and relentless self-discipline. Neither in college nor afterward did he touch drink stronger than wine, and drank wine only sparingly. At the time of his engagement to Alice Lee he noted in his private diary: "Thank heaven I am absolutely pure. I can tell Alice everything I have done."[3] Translated from mid-Victorian English this, of course, had reference to any form of sexual indulgence. And yet there are no indications that he regarded such successful self-mastery as exceptional. To him it seems to have been merely a part of a deliberate process of concentrating his energies upon building a powerful body. The fact that this process was not completed to his satisfaction until he was in his late twenties may explain the otherwise apparently pathological extremes of so many of his deeds in his Dakota days—rides of seventy miles or more in a day, hunting hikes of fourteen to sixteen hours, stretches in the saddle in roundups of as long as forty hours without surcease or sleep. Some of these were, of course, "in line of duty"—especially while moving cattle on the range. But his obvious delight in his prowess suggests that the increase in his endurance was proof to him of the success with which he was consciously shaping and strengthening himself.

While all of this, of course, happened before my day, it is my clear impression, based on my knowledge of the man, that his system of self-discipline went far beyond the traditional church teachings about self-denial and centered in a more affirmative concept—forcing himself to overcome fear, fatigue, and frustration. His control of himself was planned and constructive. By instinct he was a fighter, but never cantankerous. While he did not seek quarrels he would not shun one if he felt that it could not be honorably avoided. Typical of the few instances of his becoming involved in an actual fight in North Dakota is the case mentioned in his autobiography of a drunken bully in a bar who took exception to TR's spectacles and announced that: "Four-Eyes was going to treat." TR explained that he joined in the laugh and got behind the stove and sat down, thinking to escape notice. The bully followed him, however, and repeated his demand that "Four-Eyes" should set up the drinks. In TR's own words: "I said, 'Well, if I've got to I've got to,' and rose looking past him. As I rose I struck quick and hard with my right just to one side of the point of his jaw, hitting with my left as I straightened out, and then again with my right."[4] The man went down, and as he did so, he struck the corner of the bar with his head. TR took away his guns, and the crowd in the bar carried the man out and laid him in a shed. He never reappeared. The incident showed not only TR's fearlessness, but also his purely practical longheadedness. At the same time that he got rid of an obnoxious bully he had proved to the community that he was not afraid to fight if he had to.

This incident also illustrates another of his outstanding characteristics—his quickness in reaching a decision and in implementing it effectively. Owen Wister picked up a good story of TR's presence of mind—also in the Dakota days. While helping to catch horses in a corral before starting the roundup, a cowpuncher roped a horse that broke out of the corral and in the process caught the cowboy's foot in a twist of the rope and dragged him off at a gallop. TR instantly mounted his own horse and, galloping after the bronco, roped and halted it, thus enabling the man who was being dragged to get free from the twist of his lariat. Not only had TR's action—and reaction—been instantaneous, but when TR returned to the corral, Wister's informant asked him what he, TR, would have done if he had missed the horse when he threw his rope. TR's instant response was: "Why, I would have shot the horse, of course." Clearly it was the only thing to do to save the man's life. Yet this was the reaction not of an experienced rancher but of a novice, who, however, had the gift of seeing clearly, deciding instantly, and acting forthwith.[5]

It was his quickness in following decision with action—as he phrased it in a talk with O. K. Davis: "When I make up my mind to do a thing, I act"—which was at the bottom of much of the criticism of him as being too impulsive. In elaborating his technique, TR said to Davis: "A good many of my 'dear friends' call me impulsive and jumpy and say that I go off half-cocked, when, as a matter of fact, I have really given full consideration to whatever it is that is to be done."[6] This, be it noted, bears no relation to "impulsiveness" in the ordinary sense of the word, which, as commonly used, means doing something that is not the result of reflection. It is worth pointing out that two of the ablest of the journalists who "covered" TR through the years confirmed his own diagnosis of his mental processes. "Of all the men I have known in and out of public life," Jack Leary, who represented the *New York Tribune* and later the *Herald*, wrote, "I have known none of any consequence whatever who was more careful of his premises before moving than he."[7] And Charles Willis Thompson of the *New York Times*, wrote: "There were no doubt times when Roosevelt's action in a given case seemed impulsive, but that was because of the startling suddenness with which the thing was done; it had been carefully weighed and calculated before he sprang it on the public."[8] As one who knew both these journalists well, I can vouch for their exceptionally high standing in a profession in which the accurate assessment of the character of public men is of fundamental importance.

No one could scare or bluff TR. In political strategy he often deliberately—and successfully—made an appeal which he knew ran counter to his audience's prejudices. I remember hearing in my youth how, during the campaign of 1900 (when he was candidate for Vice-President) he was scheduled to speak in a silver mining town in Colorado and was warned by the local campaign manager not to say anything against free silver, as it might result in personal violence directed against him. The story is that when TR had been introduced to his audience, which consisted largely of workers in the silver mines, he banged his fist on the rostrum and started his speech by saying: "I have been warned that I should say nothing to you against free silver. I want you to know that I am against free silver, have always been against it, and shall always be against it." He was met with almost instant applause by an audience which, while it disagreed with him completely, yet respected his courage in saying what he believed.

His friend Jacob Riis, reporter and reformer, quoted in his volume, *Theodore Roosevelt, the Citizen*, a remark attributed by an unnamed source to George William Curtis, who had been editor of Harper's Weekly in New York in the post-Civil War days and who broke with TR when the latter supported Blaine for President in the campaign of 1884: "He will not truckle or cringe. He seems to court opposition to the point of being somewhat pugnacious. His political life will probably be a turbulent one, but he will be a figure, not a figurehead, in future developments."[9] Riis also quoted from an undated editorial in the *Wall Street Journal*, which, by its context, I assume appeared in 1904, dealing with the reasons why powerful financial interests were scheming to defeat him: "All efforts to control him through his ambition have failed. Any attempt to control him by grosser forms of bribery would, of course, be useless. Effort to move him by sophistical arguments framed by clever corporation lawyers into departure from the paths of duty and law have not succeeded." This editorial, incidentally, parallels an extract from an address by Elihu Root before the Union League Club of New York on February 3, 1904:

> Men say [of TR] he is not safe. He is not safe for the men who wish to prosecute selfish schemes to the public detriment. He is not safe for the men who wish government to be conducted with greater reference to campaign contributions than to the public good. He is not safe for the men who wish to draw the President of the United States into a corner and make whispered arrangements which they dare not have known by their constituents.[10]

TR's reaction to the attempt on his life during the 1912 campaign has sometimes been cited as illustrative of his courage. Looking back on what he told me about it I am inclined to consider it rather as an example of his complete self-control. The incident occurred in Milwaukee on October 14, 1912. On that particular evening Mrs. TR was staying with my mother in New York, and the two of them were attending a performance of Johann Strauss's operetta, *Die Fledermaus*. In my diary of that year under the date of November 4, is an account that my mother gave me the previous evening on my return to Oyster Bay after working for several months in the Progressive Party's headquarters in Massachusetts. She and Mrs. TR, the diary reads,

> were on the aisle, EKR on the inside, with two spare seats besides her. George Roosevelt [a cousin] was sitting at the other end of the row. Mother had hoped that Oliver [my brother who, with George, was working at Progressive headquarters in New York] could come too, and was consequently delighted to see him appear in the seat next to Cousin Edith. As he went by Edith she didn't look up, and it was not until he was seated that she noticed who it was. Then she leaned over and put her hand on his knee. Edith found him shaking violently. At that instant, she said, she realized what had happened, and gripped his hand firmly. Although he was trembling terribly his voice was perfectly steady as he told her that Cousin Theodore had been shot at, but not hit. Mother says that she [Edith] merely gasped and then quietly said: "You say he wasn't hurt, Oliver?" and then sent him back to make sure. He reappeared soon, and said that apparently Cousin Theodore had been scratched, but had kept on with his speech.
>
> This reassured them, and though mother wanted her to leave the theater she insisted on staying, saying that he couldn't be hurt if he went on with his speech, and that if they went to campaign headquarters they would only worry terribly.
>
> When the show was over the reporters were already on hand and George kept them away while mother and Cousin Edith went out a side entrance and took an auto for headquarters. There they found that he had actually been wounded, and Cousin Edith debated about going out to Chicago immediately, or waiting until the 20th Century [which would leave at 5:00 P.M. the next day] which she finally did. Mother says that all that night and the next day [which they spent at my mother's house] Cousin Edith was absolutely calm and self-possessed. She is a remarkable woman.

The morning after this entry was made I went up to Sagamore, where TR was recuperating from the strain and the extraction of the bullet. TR, Edith, Archie, and I sat in the library talking for an hour or more and were then joined by my mother. It was a Sunday, and as time to go to church approached, Archie brought in TR's heavy overcoat and helped him put it on. My diary reads:

The right arm was a little stiff, and Arch asked if it hurt. TR laughed and said that there was no pain, but that the muscles were still black and blue all around the spot. [This was about three weeks after the shooting.]

Archie who had walked towards the North Room, called out to me: "He says it was only like the kick of a mule."

"That's all it was," said TR.

"Well, I know what that's like"; said Arch, laughing. "I've been kicked by a mule and I never want to be again!"

"But didn't it knock you right over?" I asked.

"Yes," said TR. "It knocked me right back, but I got right up." And he then proceeded to show us just what happened. Mother and I were standing together. TR backed us off about three feet, and then said: "I was standing like this, not well braced, and had my hat raised like this"—he raised his right arm a little to show how it happened. "There were two men standing there where you two are. Schranck [the would-be assassin] put his gun between them so that no-one could see, and fired."

The force of it knocked him back, but he said that curiously enough it [the incident] didn't go to his head at all. When he got up he thought the bullet had merely hit him and glanced off, although he felt a burning sensation.

What followed happened quickly. Colonel Lyon [Cecil Lyon of Texas] TR said, was trying to clear the crowd so as to shoot the man but he couldn't get clear, and in the meantime E. E. Martin [a member of TR's party] had caught the man and brought him to TR. He was a poor weak, individual of the criminal class. Actually, however, he was not insane, but merely suffering from very low mentality.

Of Martin TR spoke glowingly because of his instantaneous action in jumping even before the shot was fired.

(A few days later I met Martin—a man with the build of a football player, pleasant, amusing, and modest. He dined with a group of us. The diary records that "he told us how he caught the gleam of Schranck's gun, and jumped as the man fired, bearing him to the ground. After a struggle he wrenched the gun away, and had the assassin at his mercy.")

When TR had finished telling us about the incident, the family left for church, and as they got into the auto TR suggested that I come back to Sagamore in the afternoon. When I got back Archie took me upstairs to look for a watch chain in TR's dressing room. The diary resumes:

> In one of the drawers of TR's bureau he found a wad of paper and suddenly exclaimed: "Oh, there's the speech!" and delving deeper brought out a spectacle case with a bullet hole through it. It was the Milwaukee speech and the steel case that deflected the assassin's bullet. The speech, done on heavy paper folded double, was pierced and badly torn. Through the spectacle case was a round hole about the size of a finger. Archie experimented to see where they would fit and we then went downstairs again.

In the meantime other relatives had arrived, and, as tea was set in motion (the diary resumes) "Cousin T. called for the speech and spectacle case and exhibited them with glee, and the most deliberate cold blood, assuring us that except for them he would now be dead."

The diary then turned to political and family subjects, but contemporary accounts of the shooting indicate that the essential thing is that after being hit by the bullet, he put his hand to his mouth, and seeing that there was no blood, he felt certain that the bullet had not penetrated the lung. He realized, of course, that he might be seriously injured, but he decided that the thing for him to do was to go ahead and to deliver his speech even if this was the last thing that he would ever do. He spoke for an hour or more, showing increasing signs of strain and exhaustion, and when it was over he had trouble getting away from the crowd of well-wishers who insisted on shaking hands with him.

Throughout his life TR was frankly proud of his achievements. To his critics this seemed not only an unpleasant weakness, but discreditable. But I think it had a simple explanation. His achievements were so much greater than he could have dared hope that his pride in them was boyishly irrepressible. He spoke of them not so much in bald egotism as in a sort of paean of incredulous self-congratulation—something comparable to a good golfer's pleased and proudly expressed surprise at having made a particularly good shot. Consider the record: When he resigned as Assistant Secretary of the Navy in 1898 to help organize the Rough Riders he hoped that his army career would be creditable and would foster his political advancement. But he could not possibly have expected that within a little more than three years he would be President of the United States. He knew that his career to date had been meteoric. He knew that he had been publicly acclaimed—and denounced—since the year after he left college, and he probably knew by then what he later publicly admitted, that he had a great gift of leadership. Of course he was ambitious. Of course he sought success in his chosen field of public life. Many people were sure that he would go far and did not hesitate to tell him so. As early as 1895 Cabot Lodge had written him that he did not preclude the possibility of TR ending up in the White House.[11] But TR knew that the chances of this happening were small, and, if ever, only in the distant future. Even when, after the Cuban War, he was nominated for governor of New York at the age of thirty-nine, he was still far from the White House. And yet when, on September 14, 1901, he succeeded to the presidency on the death of William McKinley, his forty-third birthday was still six weeks ahead. Only the success of the younger Pitt in England was more fantastic than the rise of this young American from police commissioner of New York City to President of the United States in four years. A half-century later John F. Kennedy, at forty-three, became the youngest man ever elected to the presidency.

Like all men in public life, TR loved acclaim. Even in private life he liked to be the center of things—"the bride at every wedding and the corpse at every funeral," as someone facetiously put it. And one of the reasons for this is that he played the part brilliantly. The knowledge of this skill bolstered his natural inclination to take the lead. Furthermore, people expected it of him. They came to hear him—and this was as true of persons invited to a meal as of those who attended a rally at which he spoke. And yet so rapid was his progress from one success to another that it must have been hard for him to grasp—and easy for him to exult.

It should not be overlooked that a great political leader has some of the characteristics of a great actor. In our own time this was notably true of Winston Churchill. It would not be surprising, therefore, to find that successful politicians not only thrive on applause, as do great actors, but that, like them, they suffer when deprived of this applause, and that, like great actors, they suffer even more when denied an audience. I doubt if anyone other than Mrs. Roosevelt and a very few of his close friends sensed the psychological problems that he faced when he left the presidency in 1909, just a few months over fifty years of age. Not only was he still full of torrential energy, but he knew that throughout his life he had thrived on achievement. There was a certain amount of truth in Henry Adams' characterization of TR as "pure act," a phrase which, in its context, was obviously intended to disparage.[12] TR seemed to derive strength from mere accomplishment, and in the course of his presidency he was constantly pushing reforms and seeking to attain specific goals. A good administrator, and quick to enlist the active support of intelligent assistants, his days in the White House were full of constructive activities. And yet here he was on March 4,

1909, at the peak of his maturity and in vigorous health, cut off from the office that for seven years he had used to give vent to his passion for accomplishment. Not only had the play run its course, but the star's contract had expired, the theater had been closed, and no other stage was available to the actor whose popularity had for years been phenomenal.

I doubt that he at first realized how completely he was cut off from his lifelong productive activities. The African expedition was a welcome and much needed vacation and change, and as its purpose was the collection of specimens for the natural history museum it absorbed not only his physical energy but his interested attention. It was followed by visits to the leading capitals in Europe, which, incidently, furnished the material for one of the most interesting and readable of all his published writings—his long letter to the British historian, Sir George Otto Trevelyan, with its sequel to his American friend, David Gray, both of which were subsequently printed in the small volume entitled *Cowboys and Kings.* Included also in this book was a long letter that he had written to John Hay about his hunting trips in Colorado in 1904. The letters about Europe describe vividly people whom he met and what they talked about and give an interesting picture of a world that was soon to reach the end of an era.

TR returned to the United States in the summer of 1910, a leader no longer, with nothing to do other than to try to handle an enormous unsolicited correspondence, and to write an article a week for *Outlook,* in which, out of loyalty to his successor in the White House, he refrained as long as he could from criticism. He was beset by friends and former associates who not only felt that Taft had let them—and him—down, but who sought to use him in their efforts either to advance their own interests, or to block the resurgence of reactionary Republicans in the party counsels at the national and state levels. Despite multiplications of appeals to him to intervene, he sensed that he had little influence with the leaders of the Republican machine because he no longer had the popular following that had made him such a formidable political power. He knew that the party leaders still feared—and hated—him. But he also knew that he was powerless to thwart them. The party was split, but his friends, almost without exception, had little influence in the party organization. A less combative man might have turned to melancholy and self-pity. But it was out of character for TR to take things lying down. By late summer in 1910 he concluded that he owed it to his friends to do what he could in New York State to check the power of the reactionary Republican leaders, foremost among whom was William Barnes, Jr. At the Republican state convention gathered to nominate a candidate for governor he was elected temporary chairman, defeating the Old Guard's candidate for that post, James S. Sherman, then Vice-President of the United States. The convention nominated TR's candidate for Governor, Henry L. Stimson, a man of ability and high character, but who proved to be a poor campaigner. Owing to his lack of voter appeal and to the fact that the party machine leaders were reluctant to see a Roosevelt man in the governorship, their support of Mr. Stimson was cool. He was defeated by upwards of 60,000 votes and shortly thereafter was appointed Secretary of War by President Taft—an office that he filled with distinction, as he did his later cabinet posts under Hoover and FDR.

The outcome of the election of 1910 not only in New York State but throughout the country made it clear that the Republican Party was neither as strong as it had been while TR was President, nor as unified. The Republicans lost control of the House of Representatives. Insurgent Republicans battled reactionaries in many states. The old-line machine politicians of course were determined to cling to their control of the party organization. They disliked the type of reforms for which various groups of progressives and insurgents clamored, but, above all, their main interest was in preventing liberal Republicans from infiltrating the party organizations, local, state, and national.

The resulting situation was difficult for TR. All his life he had been a straight organization man. But his sympathies had always been with the reforming and liberal elements of the party, and he had repeatedly fought and deplored the ties between the machine and big business leaders. While I have no documentary evidence to support my guess I think that in 1910 he felt that the Old Guard was so determined to prevent his return to a position of influence in the party—let alone a position of power—that their attitude seemed to him a sort of personal affront, a challenge not only to his combative soul, but even to his elemental right to stand up and be counted in Republican affairs. After all, for seven and a half years he had been the titular head of the Republican Party, and an immensely popular Republican President. The least that he had a right to expect was that the party leaders would treat him as a sort of "elder statesmen"—despite his relative youth. But the Old Guard leaders as early as 1910 made it plain that they would ignore him, and hoped to muzzle him. As the great game of politics was then played in this country this was a logical—and not unexpected—attitude. But what the reactionary leaders failed to realize was that such an attitude on their part made it harder than ever for him to stay on the sidelines. If he behaved as they wished him to he would be surrendering his principles as well as his independence of action. He was a fighter at heart, and he believed that if he failed to support the elements in the party that stood for the things which he had long advocated, he would, in effect, be betraying his friends and abandoning his principles. Silence and inaction would be interpreted as surrender to the leaders of reaction. Given these circumstances he would not have been true to himself had he not used all his skill, his courage and his persistence in helping his political friends and espousing the progressive principles in which he believed.

8

THE POWER OR THE GLORY?

HISTORIANS TEND to blame TR for the split in the Republican Party in 1912 and to ascribe his candidacy for the presidency in that year to an insatiable "lust for power." To one who saw much of him throughout 1912 this facile judgment seems unfair on at least two counts: 1) It assumes that it was he who caused the split in the party, whereas the party had been largely unified by him in the seven years that he was in the White House and only split when he left office. The split resulted from the determination of the reactionary elements, particularly those in both houses of Congress, to punish the Republican insurgents for their independence. 2) It interprets as a hunger for power what was, in fact, a desire to further policies and reforms in which TR deeply believed and which could only be achieved through active support on his part of the liberal and progressive elements in the Republican Party.

My initial impressions of what happened in 1912 were colored by my associations with TR. But during the last half-century I have read and thought much about that campaign, and by interpreting what I have read in the light of my knowledge of the man and of what I saw of the campaign from the inside, I think that I can throw light on some of his reactions, decisions, and acts during that critical year. I was a sophomore at Harvard in the spring of 1912, and politically inexperienced. But after rereading the diary that I kept that year, which included my attendance at the Republican National Convention, I realize that I was an alert observer.

From what I saw and heard in 1912 I am convinced that TR entered the race with reluctance, and then only when he was sure that the majority of the Republican voters wanted him to do so. I am also convinced that he underestimated the stubborn resolution of the reactionary Republican leaders to prevent his being nominated—a determination that stiffened as evidences of strong popular support for TR increased in early 1912. The reason for this opposition was that his return to office with a large popular following would jeopardize the Old Guard's domination of the party machinery as well as the formulation and execution of party policies. Almost without exception the Republican machine leaders viewed TR not merely with suspicion but with aversion. They had distrusted him as vice-presidential candidate and disliked him when he was in the White House. His immense popularity gave him strength and independence as President and his political shrewdness made him hard to control. Many of them would have liked to prevent his nomination to succeed himself in 1904 and were irked by the size of the popular vote for him in that election.

When finally the fourth of March dawned in 1909 their relief was unmistakable. It is true that the new President had been imposed on the party by TR, and some of them feared that Mr. Taft might try to follow too closely in TR's footsteps. But it didn't take long for them to learn that the new President was friendly, easygoing, and anxious to cooperate. With TR off to Africa for a year to hunt lions the Old Guard leaders took a rosy look at the world again, and even smiled when cartoonists and quipsters elaborated the obvious tag: "Mr. Taft expects every lion to do its duty!"

This African trip was ostensibly for the collecting of animal specimens for the Smithsonian Institute and the Museum of Natural History in New York. So successful was it as a dramatic and picturesque undertaking that people—including historians—have tended to overlook one of its basic purposes, which was to enable TR to get so far out of reach that neither directly nor indirectly could anyone charge that he was trying to guide or influence Taft in his conduct of the presidency. When TR picked Taft as his successor he believed him to be well equipped for that post. TR wished to leave Mr. Taft completely on his own, realizing that if he (TR) were within reach of journalists and politicians during the first months of Taft's administration these men would be constantly trying to enlist either his support for, or his opposition to, Taft's acts. He believed that the President should be the center of American political life, and he was glad that he had turned over to Taft a party organization that was more harmonious than it had been for years. TR took pride in the fact that this harmony was in large measure the result of his own efforts to bring about better relations between the conservative and liberal elements in the party. Furthermore, he believed that Taft would carry on the policies that he had helped TR initiate.

Yet when TR returned from Africa and his European tour in June, 1910, he found the Republican Party torn asunder. As George E. Mowry pointed out in his book, *Theodore Roosevelt and the Progressive Movement,* TR's part in unifying the Republican Party before he left office had given him an artist's pride in his own creation. Inevitably, as Mowry put it, a "sense of irritation grew against the man who, he reasoned, had destroyed it."[1] The more TR heard and read about Taft's lack of leadership and his submission to the reactionaries in the party the more evident it became that Taft had not filled the bill as TR had hoped and had assured the country that he would. The knowledge that he, TR, was responsible for Taft being in the White House must have plagued him. No one enjoys having openly endorsed a friend for a job and seeing that friend fail to live up to expectations. I have not found direct evidence, either in print or in my own manuscript diaries, to support the idea that TR admitted being chagrined by Taft's failure, but there is a pertinent sentence in my diary under date of May 20, 1912, at the end of a discussion between TR's son Archie and myself about the progress of the campaign, which reads as follows: "As Archie says—one of TR's greatest blunders was in advocating Taft." Surely if we youngsters sensed this at the time, TR could not have been unaware of this fundamental truth. Certainly if he knew it this might explain some of the bitterness that later crept into his remarks about Taft. TR was a proud man and also clear-eyed and honest. If, as I suspect, he realized the nature of his misjudgment, this could have been galling to his pride, as well as disillusioning.

That TR had been mistaken about Taft is easily understandable. Taft had been a loyal and efficient lieutenant in posts of importance, such as governor of the Philippines and Secretary of War. Later he served with distinction as a member of the Supreme Court of the United States. But Taft lacked the qualities of a successful politician—and the presidency is the greatest political office in the world. He had no gift for leadership or for forceful and dramatic self-expression and was reluctant to fight—or even to disagree with—political adversaries. Conservative by inclination, he easily—and probably unconsciously—came to depend on the reactionary leaders in the Republican Party—men whose first interest was to control the party machinery and whose concern about legislation was that it should not embarrass or displease the rich and powerful from whom campaign funds should flow. By openly aligning himself with the Old Guard, Taft reopened the rift in the Republican Party which TR thought he had healed.

During the summer of 1910 and all through 1911 TR continued to try to restore party harmony and declared in his letters to friends and supporters that he expected to endorse Taft. The letters, of course, were critical of Taft from time to time, but they do not show until the end of December, 1911, that TR was seriously considering seeking the nomination in the coming national convention.

What, then, brought about the change in his point of view?

The usual explanation has been, as I suggested in the opening paragraph of this chapter, that he was power-hungry—that he had an irresistible urge to get back into the White House. Even as perceptive a biographer as W. H. Harbaugh speaks of TR's "vaulting personal ambition."[2] I believe that both phrases—"hunger for power" and "vaulting personal ambition"—are misinterpretations of TR's character. This may be partly because the word *power* has acquired an ugly connotation since the days of Mussolini, Stalin, Hitler, and their successors, who sought and obtained unlimited power and used it for their selfish ends. As now applied to TR the word suggests that he, like these men, had a compelling urge to rule. It seems to me more accurate to say that TR was more interested in effecting constructive reforms than in holding office. Insofar as he had any strong "compulsion" it was for achievement—for getting things done. This is borne out in the memorandum that Judge Robert Grant of Boston sent to the historian James Ford Rhodes about a long talk that the Judge had with TR the evening before TR announced his decision to be a candidate in 1912. To the direct question from Judge Grant: "You would like to be President?" TR replied: "I like power. But I care nothing to be President as President. I am interested in these ideas of mine and I want to carry them through, and I feel that I am the one to carry them through."[3] Of course he had enjoyed the presidency. But repeatedly during the years since he had left the White House he insisted to his intimates that he had nothing to gain by another term. As he put it to his son Theodore, Jr. on December 26, 1911, "For me personally the nomination would be a veritable calamity."[4] A few weeks later he wrote to Frank Munsey: "From every personal standpoint there is nothing for me to gain either in running for the office or in holding the office once more, and there is very much to lose."[5] Over and over again he had said the same thing to friends, relatives, and strangers. But as TR had said to Judge Grant, he was deeply concerned about his "ideas" —a fact that William Roscoe Thayer, who was present at the judge's interview with TR, summarized by saying: "He felt more passionately than anybody else the need of continuing the work which he had begun—not because it was his work, but because on it alone, as he thought, the reconciliation between capital and labor in the United States could be brought about and the impending war of the classes could be prevented."[6] Further confirmation of this is to be found in a diary entry of mine dated April 28, 1912, recording what my mother had told me about what TR had told her the same day at lunch: "He said he didn't want another term, but it appears now that he feels there are certain things that he can accomplish, and which must be accomplished, which he feels Taft could never tackle." The parallel is so close to what TR had told Judge Grant two months earlier, and the fact that he spoke to the judge as he did to my mother and to Archie and myself with complete frankness and with no need for any kind of dissimulation or caution adds validity to the estimate that this truly expressed his sentiments at the time. Indubitably he had in him a lust for achievement—a lust for the attainment of specific objectives. But it is far from clear that he had what could fairly be called a lust for power.

Consider two specific incidents in his career:

The first is his statement made on the night of the election in 1904 to the effect that under no circumstances would he accept another nomination. The statement was obviously made in full sincerity, and in the belief that it would strengthen his position during the succeeding four years in the White House. It turned out to have been a political blunder, because it played directly into the hands of the reactionary leaders in the party, who, already in November of 1904, were determined to prevent this "madman" from obtaining another term in 1908. Had he kept the party leaders guessing as to whether or not he would seek the nomination in 1908, their capacity for obstruction would have been lessened and he almost surely could have accomplished more and would have become a greater power in the party. But the moment he said that he would not accept another nomination the Old Guard leaders ceased to fear him.

A rereading of the events preceding the convention of 1908 makes it plain that TR could have had the nomination in 1908 in spite of this self-denying declaration. Surely if he had been as power-mad as his detractors claim, he would never have made such a self-denying declaration nor would he have forced the Republican convention in 1908 to name his friend and follower William Howard Taft as his successor. Instead, he would have used the enormous political influence of the presidency between November of 1904 and June of 1908 to insure his own renomination at the convention in 1908, which could have been—and, in fact, was—completely dominated by his friends and henchmen. The distinction which TR later made—and that his foes branded as a sort of disingenuous afterthought—that there was a difference between a President seeking more than two terms in succession and a former President seeking a third term after being out of office—was based on thorough knowledge of the actual working of the political machinery of the American party system. A President in office, even at the end of his second term, can exercise very much more influence over political agents than can a former President who has been out of office for a term or more. As TR's distant kinsman later proved, a President could —and actually did—have himself reelected three times after his initial taking of office.

The second pertinent factor bearing on his so-called "vaulting ambition" was the speech that he made in Columbus, Ohio, only a few days before formally announcing his candidacy for the nomination in 1912. This was the speech in which he advocated the recall of judicial decisions. As he explained it on various occasions, the recall of judicial decisions meant that if a court declares an act of the legislature to be unconstitutional the people shall have the right to say whether the legislature or the court shall be held best to have interpreted their wishes. It was the opinion of his close friends and admirers at the time—and since—that this speech alienated many middle-of-the-road Republicans who might otherwise have supported him. Nothing else that he said throughout the entire campaign did so much to consolidate the opposition of right-wingers and moderates. The speech was not a casual, half-baked product. It had been prepared weeks in advance and had been checked by distinguished jurists. It expressed views that were consistent with many of his theories of liberal reforms. To such a shrewd and experienced politician as TR it must have been clear that this speech might hurt him. It is hard to see how a "power-hungry" man could have deliberately injected into his bid for office an issue that was so likely to lose him so much support—as, in fact, it did.

If it was not power that he sought, was it glory?

This, also, I question. He had had his full measure of glory and had loved every minute of it. But TR was a practical man. He knew that if elected in 1912 he would have to work with and through men who had long hated him and who would be particularly bitter thenceforth not only because he had upset their control of the party, but also because he would be pressing political and social reforms that they abhorred. To be President again would be a tough assignment, and while he never flinched from a responsibility because it might be unpleasant, he knew that the strain on him, physical as well as mental, would be great. He was beginning to feel his age, even though relatively young (he would be fifty-four just before the November election). The novelty of being President had worn off long before, and he knew that great as had been his popularity when he was in the White House, such popularity was at best fickle—as quickly withdrawn as given. On balance the disadvantages outweighed the glory.

Why, then, did he decide to run?

The only explanation that strikes me as in keeping with his character was his strong sense of obligation—obligation to his friends and to those who believed in his policies of reform. Not that he looked on himself as the "indispensable man." Rather was he the most available man to lead the cause in which he—and many Americans—deeply believed. Through the first six weeks of 1912 evidence piled up that popular support for him was strong and widespread. Some of the progressives—particularly in Wisconsin and Minnesota—were partisans of Senator Robert M. LaFollette, but as LaFollette stood for many of the same kind of reforms that TR advocated there was no unhealable doctrinal split between the two progressive groups. But LaFollette's personal following was much smaller than TR's, both numerically and geographically. Outside of the few states in the Midwest in which LaFollette was dominant, the reports that came to TR from trusted and experienced advisers made it clear that if the delegates to the national convention could be chosen by popular vote, TR would have an easy majority. The difficulty lay in the fact that in only a quarter of the states were the delegates at that time chosen in primary elections. In the rest—and particularly in the southern states—the delegates were hand-picked by the party machine leaders. In 1908 the delegates from the southern states had dutifully voted as TR wished—for Taft. In 1912 they again supported Taft—under orders from Taft's campaign managers. In other words, a President in office has a hard core of hand-picked delegates who can be relied upon to follow the orders of the Republican National Committee and the convention officials from start to finish.

By way of elaboration there is an entry in my diary under date of April 14, 1912, reading:

We lunched today at Sagamore, and my brother and I cornered TR and cross-questioned him about the political situation. He explained the delegate system, and said that if it could only be honestly carried out he would favor it more than the direct primary. But as this is practically impossible he wants the direct primary as the lesser of two evils. In the South the delegate system is absolutely in the hands of the administration. But he says that the delegates don't count for much, and are mostly uninstructed. Nevertheless the system is all machine-controlled. It is this system that he was fighting in Illinois and Pennsylvania. With characteristic confidence he remarked that if the people of the country could vote as they felt, he would have four-fifths of the country. But the bosses control everything.

The details of the primary battles in the thirteen states in which they were held have little interest in these distant days. The significant thing is that in the states holding primaries TR's lead was so large as to make it clear beyond any possible question that he was the choice of many more Republican voters than was Taft. According to Mowry, in the thirteen states where the rank and file of Republicans voted in 1912 TR received 278 delegates, Taft 48, and LaFollette 36. In the popular vote in these states TR received more than Taft and LaFollette combined.[7]

But because of the delegate system in the thirty-five states that did not have primaries, the Taft forces went into the convention with a large number of pledged delegates who could be relied upon to follow the orders of the national committee and the convention officials without any danger of their defecting to Roosevelt. This gave Taft a substantial lead, but not an absolute majority. Everything depended, therefore, on what happened to the contested delegates—contests that had arisen in a number of states where a slate of delegates was pledged to Taft and another to Roosevelt. It was up to the Credentials Committee of the Republican National Committee to decide the contests. Estimates vary as to the minimum number of contested delegates that TR would have to win in order to control the convention. George Mowry, whose study of the Progressive movement appears to have been thorough, stated that probably about one hundred Roosevelt contests deserved a careful examination and added pointedly: "From the investigations of these contests it was obvious that the committee as a whole was less interested in justice than in seating enough delegates pledged to Taft to insure his nomination."[8] He further particularized that "it would seem that Roosevelt had a right to at least thirty more delegates than he received."[9] Mowry then went on to explain that while thirty additional votes would not have given TR control of the convention, these additional thirty delegates, together with a few for Senator Albert B. Cummins of Iowa and for LaFollette, would have enabled TR to dictate the organization of the convention and to block Taft's victory on the first ballot.[10] Out of 254 contests 235 were decided in favor of Taft and 19 in favor of Roosevelt.[11] All of which lends credence to the view which those of us who attended the convention held at the time—that the nomination was stolen from TR by the Taft forces. Most of the actual thefts were described as the result of "steamroller tactics," which gives added zest to a genially mixed metaphor that I found in my diary under date of June 14: "The steamroller has been working in a most disgraceful manner, stealing delegates and proving its infamy."

9

A NEW PARTY IS BORN

THE NATIONAL REPUBLICAN CONVENTION in Chicago in 1912 was due to open on June 18. As late as June 12 TR had not decided whether he should go to Chicago to take charge of the drive for his nomination. On the thirteenth I gathered from his son Kermit that he would probably go. As I planned to go with him I left Cambridge for Oyster Bay, and early on the morning of June 14 I went up to Sagamore for breakfast and found TR, his wife, and their daughter Ethel at the table. As we sat there, dispatches were brought in from time to time, and TR was unusually silent. Cousin Edith clearly dreaded going to Chicago, but he was considering it because it seemed that his private telephone to Chicago was being tapped.

At about 9 A.M. he and Edith got into their automobile to drive to New York. As they were leaving he called out to me: "Well, Nick, I guess we'll meet at a lot of Philippics soon." And then he added: "But we may hurry back here tonight, and, by gracious, I hope we do!"

His hope was not realized. At noon his office in New York telephoned to Sagamore to say that he was leaving for Chicago on the Lake Shore Limited at 5:30 P.M. I took the first train to New York and bought a ticket on the Lake Shore Limited, and Kermit and I waited at the gate for other members of the party. We were soon joined by our cousin, George Roosevelt (the oldest son of Emlen Roosevelt), former Governor Regis Post of Puerto Rico, and two members of the staff of *Outlook.* Shortly before 5:30 P.M. TR and Cousin Edith were brought to the train by a side approach so as to avoid attention.

Scarcely had we been gone an hour when there was considerable crashing and banging, and the train came to a sudden stop. The locomotive had struck a boulder, but no serious damage had been done. As an omen it could be regarded as either good or bad.

Early the next morning, when the train stopped at Elkhart, Indiana, Walter Brown, the Ohio manager of TR's campaign, came on board, and about a half-hour later, at South Bend, John Callan O'Laughlin of the *Chicago Tribune*, who had been scheduled to be TR's secretary if and when the campaign was successful, joined us, bringing optimistic reports. As O'Laughlin and I were sitting in the smoker discussing these reports TR joined us and spoke about his general plan. My diary reads:

The main points were, briefly, that he had come to fight and to win, and that a bolt would be worked, but only in the very last extremities. Everything must be done to prevent a bolt—everything possible —and if there were one, it must appear regular and unbolt-like. Probably none would be necessary, as Taft, with all contests included, could not muster more than 536 votes [out of a total of 1078]. . . . All the news was of the best, and TR was bubbling with cheerfulness. Once more he remarked what so few will believe: "You know," said he, "I think—and I mean this seriously—I really think that there has never before been a campaign waged on such high principles. We have reached a crisis in the history of this country . . " He then suddenly left us and went back to his compartment.

The diary continues:

By this time we were approaching Chicago, and everything was got in readiness to leave. It was rumored that there would be a crowd. We finally drew in, and under instructions to keep tight with the old man, he led the way and we followed. The crowd had broken through the police lines and were packed on the platform, yelling and cheering and surging around. With Teddy Douglas Robinson [his nephew] taking one arm and Frank Harper [secretary to TR] taking the other, and George Roosevelt and I behind, we managed to wedge our way through this shrieking mob out into the street, which was a sea of cheering people. With much difficulty we forced our way into one of the special autos, and there followed one of the most thrilling events of my life. People packed the windows and lined the roofs, and were so thick in the streets we could hardly move in the procession. Everyone was howling with delight, and cries of "Teddy!" filled the air. At the cross streets as far as we could see to either side people were wedged in. Everyone cheered, everyone was hurled along in the irresistible force of the delighted mob. Ahead rode TR bowing to right and to left while the cheering continued.

During the ensuing eight days I had a closeup of one of the most interesting conventions in our history. I attended all but one of the meetings of the Roosevelt delegates discussing strategy. I had brief talks with TR almost daily, and took notes of his off-the-record talks to the Roosevelt delegates. When the convention officially opened I sat through all its sessions, and when it closed, after nominating Taft, I attended the meeting of the 344 Roosevelt delegates who had refused to vote at the official convention. The copy of the diary that I kept at the convention, to which I added extracts from letters that I wrote home at the time and from notes which I kept at the meetings, runs into fifty-three typed pages. Much of it deals with people long since forgotten and with events, plans, and rumors which today are of no interest except to a handful of researchers delving into obscure facets of American party politics.

Then, as now, national political conventions combined aspects of a circus with those of a public dinner honoring a celebrity. Lacking were only the animals and the food. The drama and the speeches were carefully planned in advance. In theory the delegates met to choose a candidate. In fact they usually merely ratified a choice made in the preceding weeks or months by a small number of party leaders behind closed doors. If a deadlock occurred while the convention was in session, it was nearly always settled by a handful of leaders. Usually two or more candidates were permitted to enter the field, backed by different groups of politicians, which sometimes led to last-minute trading and deals. Thus by the time a convention met everything was organized, and the favorite of the political leaders was put across in such a manner as to make him seem to be the popular choice.

What the leaders wanted was, above all else, a probable winner. This meant that he must either be already popular or have the gift of developing personal popularity. In the next place, he must be either a good politician, or amenable to political guidance. They had no objections to a nonprofessional, such as Herbert Hoover or Dwight D. Eisenhower, so long as there was little likelihood that he would and could seek to exercise power. The professionals' ideal candidate was a man like Warren Gamaliel Harding (who, incidentally, made the nominating speech for Taft in 1912)—an amiable insider, trained by politicians as a politician, "reasonable" (i.e., always glad to oblige his political associates) "sensible" (i.e., ready to have others do his thinking and make his decisions for him). A candidate should, if possible, be photogenic. As tastes change this means that in the prebeatnik bearded age, Benjamin Harrison's well-groomed, ample whiskers gave him a look of dependability. Later, William Howard Taft's copious form and genial countenance made people believe that he must be reliable. Harding's somewhat Indian-like appearance gave the impression that in the event of trouble, he would know what to do. Eisenhower was boyish-looking in an innocent way, unaffected and friendly. If Nixon had not looked so grim, dour and coal-dusted, he might well have beaten John F. Kennedy.

Because at the convention of 1912, the party was split into two powerful, irreconcilable factions, the activities behind the scenes were hectic. As late as the day we left New York for Chicago (June 14) TR's information was, as I have indicated, that Taft could not muster more than 536 out of the 1078 delegates. At this time approximately eighty delegates were still in dispute, which means that there were at least eighty instances in which there was a contest between a man pledged to Taft and one pledged to Roosevelt.

As I noted in the previous chapter, one of the most careful recent students of the 1912 convention, George E. Mowry, estimated that at least thirty of the Roosevelt delegates who had been rejected by the Old Guard forces, should probably have been seated. Had this happened, TR would almost surely have been nominated—which the Taft managers knew just as well as did the Roosevelt managers. It was because of this that the contests were so important. How these contests were, in fact, decided, may be gleaned from a reference in my diary to what Elon Huntington Hooker told TR in my presence when he described his appearance before the Credentials Committee in behalf of the Roosevelt delegates contested in Mississippi: "Everyone was walking around and smoking, and there was so much noise no one could hear. He [Hooker] was allowed fifteen minutes to present what it had taken him half a day to grasp by deep study, and the committee had fifteen minutes in which to reply. Due to the noise they couldn't hear, and naturally decided the way they themselves had been directed to swing, namely, for the machine."

TR was further handicapped during this campaign by the fact that even at the time of his announcement in February, 1912, that he would be a candidate he was already cut off from —or, to be more accurate, blackballed by—the machine politicians throughout the country. Even Senator Henry Cabot Lodge of Massachusetts, who had been for years TR's shrewdest and most loyal adviser, opposed his candidacy and most of his objectives. Of the men who had been close to him when he was in the White House, only James R. Garfield and Gifford Pinchot supported him vigorously, and neither was the equal in political skill of the Taft managers. Among other Republican leaders of more than purely local stature who favored his nomination on the Republican ticket and later joined the Progressive Party were Hiram W. Johnson, governor of California, and Walter R. Stubbs, governor of Kansas. Two other Kansans, Henry J. Allen, who later was governor and senator, and William Allen White, the nationally famous editor of the *Emporia Gazette*, remained close to TR throughout the entire campaign. Of the others who went along until the break the two best known were Herbert S. Hadley, governor of Missouri, and Senator William E. Borah of Idaho. It is significant that none of these prominent Republicans was what can be described as a "machine politician." None was of national stature or influence. Among active collaborators with little political training but with considerable organizational experience were the two New York businessmen, Elon Huntington Hooker, mentioned above, and George W. Perkins, one-time Morgan partner.

The ablest professional among them was William Flinn of Pennsylvania, who had recently won control of the Pennsylvania machine from Senator Boies Penrose, who with former Senator "Don" Cameron, had long dominated Republican patronage in Pennsylvania. Flinn stands out in my memory as a man of obvious force and drive, with only a few of the traditional earmarks of the professional politician in that period. The one that I remember best was his habit of perpetually chewing the stub of a cigar. He was a handsome man of Irish extraction who might have been mistaken for a successful lawyer or businessman almost anywhere in the country at that time. He had the merit of being fundamentally and basically practical—that is, he used the means necessary to achieve a desired end. It was he, for example, who had lined up the large and influential delegation from Pennsylvania, which was the most important among the thirteen state delegations then elected by the primary system. In the diary I find under date of April 14 (two months before the convention met) that in a visit to Oyster Bay in which I saw TR, he was "delighted and much surprised about the Pennsylvania victory. It was brought about in the following manner: [I paraphrase TR's words] Flinn mailed over a million return postals asking the voters which of the Republican candidates they preferred. The answers, netting a huge majority for TR, were printed on another set of postals and sent out. Finally a third set of postals was sent out, with extracts from TR's policies. The result was a swamping victory."

I have read and reread the thousands of words of the diary that I kept while at the convention, and from them it is clear that the majority of the Roosevelt delegates believed—as did TR—that the nomination was stolen from them. The great question for all of them was—what to do about it?

Everything depended, of course, on TR. Did he want to bolt? Was he willing to do so? If he bolted was there even a possibility of his being elected? If not, what, if anything, was to be gained by bolting, either for himself or his supporters or the policies that he advocated?

I do not have any written records of his views about these questions other than the already known facts that even before he reached Chicago he was considering the possibility of leaving the party, and that, when it became apparent that he was going to be defrauded of the nomination he made it plain that he was prepared to do so, and that he hoped his supporters, or at least most of them, would go along with him. Obviously there was no point in his bolting if his supporters opposed it. Also there was no point for them to abandon the Republican Party if he would not accept the nomination on a new party ticket.

Why, then, did he decide to bolt?

In contrast to the repeated assertion of his critics that he lusted for power and that when denied the nomination by the

Republicans, he eagerly sought the nomination of the Progressive Party because he thought that this might make it possible for him to get back into the White House, my diary makes it plain that he knew that his chances of being elected on a new party ticket were practically nil. He knew better than did most of his supporters that the technical difficulties of launching a third party on a nationwide scale were practically insurmountable, owing to the fact that each state had its own election laws, including the entering of names of candidates on ballots. How is it possible to read into a decision to go open-eyed into a hopeless cause the motive of hunger for power?

We are driven, therefore, to consider other possible motives.

It has been suggested that he was vindictive—that he wanted to get even with those who had defrauded him. A lesser—or a weaker—man might have done so. But TR had little meanness in his makeup. His instincts were to be fair to an opponent, even though he could—and usually would—be ruthless while still engaged in a fight. He scorned many of his foes, but he did not harbor grudges. Once he had taught an opponent a lesson he was ready to extend the hand of friendship. It was only those who stubbornly persisted in what he was sure was error whom he hounded mercilessly. But to withdraw from a fight when he believed that he was in the right, and, in particular, when he considered that the fight had been forced on him by men who lacked candor and principles, was alien to his character. All his life he had been a fighter, and remained one. Combativeness was one of his dominant traits. There is shrewdness in Elihu Root's elaboration of this in March, 1912: "When he gets into a fight he is completely dominated by his desire to destroy his adversary. He instinctively lays hold of every weapon which can be used for that end."[1] The reactionary Republican leaders were defrauding him of the nomination and expecting him to knuckle under. He knew that if he were to abandon the contest at the Republican convention he would be playing into their hands and at the same time would be letting down his liberal friends and abandoning the policies for which he had so vigorously campaigned. Under the circumstances he saw no alternative other than to repudiate the decision of this packed and manipulated convention. It was against his nature to back out of a fight, regardless of the odds. In fact, he actually enjoyed a good fight and was cheerful even in defeat. A diary entry shows that after the Republican convention had nominated Taft and 344 of the Roosevelt delegates had refused to vote, I had a brief talk with TR "who, as usual, was irresistibly cheerful. He was delighted with the results and felt that the nomination of Sherman as Vice-President was to our advantage." Beaten by the Republican bosses and facing sure defeat on a third-party ticket, he yet was resilient and buoyant. It is pertinent to add the testimony of Governor Hiram W. Johnson, who was chairman of a meeting of the Roosevelt delegates after they had withdrawn from the convention and who said—again I quote from my diary based on notes that I took on the spot—"The cause meant more to TR than it did to any other man. We have become indignant. Yet throughout all this crisis he has never lost his dignity, his good humor or his fighting spirit."

This leads to yet another possible explanation of his motivation—that even though he knew he could not win, he realized that as a candidate on a new party ticket he could continue to get publicity for the reforms in which he believed.

His friend and associate, William Draper Lewis, Dean of the Law School of the University of Pennsylvania, who was in close touch with him at the time, gives a pertinent sidelight on this aspect of the problem. Starting out by saying that no one can understand and rightly judge TR's political actions who does not realize that he was always more interested in the message that he was delivering than in his own political fortunes, he quotes a statement that TR made to a small group who had from the start of the contest been closely associated with him: "If we form a third party and go out and fight for better social conditions in this country we will accomplish more in three months than could be accomplished under ordinary conditions in a dozen years."[2] To this Dean Lewis adds an observation of his own which I think states the case as accurately as has ever been done: "The one thing which had no influence was his desire to be President. The Progressive Party, so far as he was concerned, was founded and carried on not to put him in the White House, but to produce those changes in the machinery of government which would give the people more direct control over their State and national governments to make it impossible for small groups to override the will of the people, and to bring forward a definite, constructive program of social and economic reform."[3]

For the Roosevelt delegates the choice was by no means so clear and simple. Most of them faced a choice of three obvious courses: 1) To protest and then return to the fold, still party members, but no longer in good standing; 2) To protest and refuse to vote in the convention, which would present the Republican Party with public evidence of internal dissension and which would automatically result in the loss of all further favors for the protestors from the machine leaders; and, 3) To bolt and form a new party.

To protest and then submit was, of course, the most logical procedure. But this, as TR pointed out in one of his off-the-record talks to the Roosevelt delegates, was just what Penrose, Barnes, and the other Old Guard leaders wanted: "A number of technically honest men," he said at a private meeting of the delegates on the evening of June 21 that I attended, "assisted leaders more strictly technical to commit these outrages [the theft of the delegates] thinking we would protest and then lie down, and let them do what they want. . . . Mr. Barnes enjoys nothing more than seeing his man lie down and stay there. We will not lie down. I won't submit to being swindled by the politicians out of the people's victory. They stole all that was necessary. . . .

But if a man steal a pair of horses from you, do you expect to be satisfied if he brings you back one and says he has no use for it?"[4] Incidentally, it was at the end of another talk just like this that I noted in the diary that as he was leaving, someone gave him a rabbit's foot for good luck. According to the diary "He delightedly held it up and cried: 'A rabbit's foot! The hind foot of a Pennsylvania rabbit, killed in a graveyard in the dark of the moon.' "

TR was, of course, fully as aware as any of his supporters of the risk to a delegate's political future that necessarily inhered in refusal to abide by the decision of the national convention. As a matter of fact, he had himself faced just such a crisis in his own career in 1884 when he headed the New York State delegation to the Republican National Convention in Chicago. He, like many other delegates to that convention, not only ardently supported Senator George F. Edmunds of Vermont, but also felt that James G. Blaine, who was finally nominated, was the least promising vote-getter among the candidates presented to that convention. Many delegates were so dissatisfied with the selection of Blaine that they refused to support him. Blaine's nomination was particularly bitterly attacked by liberal Republicans who had supported TR in his fight against party bosses in Albany.

When TR finally announced that he expected to vote for Blaine he brought on himself the kind of bitter criticism that had been directed against Henry Cabot Lodge by his Massachusetts friends and clubmates when he, too, came out in support of Blaine. Both of these then young politicians supported Blaine not because they favored him but because they felt strongly that as party leaders at the convention it was their obligation to abide by the clear and unquestioned choice of that body. In an interview in the *Boston Herald* printed on July 19, 1884, TR explained his course of action clearly: "A man cannot act both without and within the party. He can do either, but he cannot possibly do both. Each course has its advantages, and each has its disadvantages, and one cannot take the advantages or the disadvantages separately. I went in with my eyes open to do what I could within the party. I did my best and got beaten; and I propose to stand by the result." He then went on to explain that Blaine had met with two checks—one at the New York State convention and the other in Chicago—"I had a hand in both," said TR, "and I could have had a hand in neither had not those Republicans who at Utica elected me as the head of the New York state delegation supposed that I would in good faith support the man who was fairly made the Republican nominee." He ended with the statement that whatever good he had been able to accomplish in public life had been accomplished through the Republican Party. "I have acted with it in the past and wish to act with it in the future," he said. "I went as a regular delegate to the Chicago convention and I intend to abide by the outcome of that convention."[5] After watching American party politics closely for more than half a century, I am of the opinion that if TR had run out on the party in 1884, his political career would have been finished then and there.

His support of Blaine in 1884 did not imply an endorsement of Blaine's character and fitness. It rested on the simple proposition that Blaine was the choice of a large majority of an open convention, after a fair struggle of other contenders to be nominated. In 1912 TR's refusal to accept the nomination of Taft was not a reflection on Taft's personal uprightness, but rather on the conviction that Taft's nomination had been achieved through fraud. TR was fully aware that his refusal to accept the nomination of Taft presented his followers with a difficult choice. Those who acquiesced in this fraud would be discredited in the eyes of many of their friends, but if they bolted they would sacrifice their political future.

My diary makes it plain that some of the most influential leaders of the Roosevelt forces, as well as most of their followers, were prepared to bolt. As early as June 18 I recorded that Governor Johnson, addressing a private meeting of the Roosevelt delegates at which I was present, said: " 'You may not realize that history has been made in that little room [where he and TR had been conferring]. I have just come from a conference with TR,' " he said, and after praising TR's leadership, he went on to say that he, Johnson, "was prepared to follow TR to the end, bolt or no bolt, and would the gentlemen agree? When he reached this point they shouted their assent and Johnson urged them to stand back of TR through thick and thin, to stand for honesty, to refuse to abide by theft, and to save the Republican party." On the next day, June 19, Flinn of Pennsylvania also came out in favor of an immediate bolt.

But as was inevitable, a number of the TR supporters did not feel that they could risk a bolt. At the time we criticized them. In retrospect I respect their decision. The outstanding cases were Governor Herbert S. Hadley of Missouri and Senator Borah of Idaho. Hadley had elements of bigness—a balanced mind, integrity, intelligence, tolerance, and a large measure of personal magnetism. He fought for TR as a Republican, but could not join the new party. Borah, more parochial and egotistical—an obstructionist rather than a doer or a creator—abandoned his support of the ideas for which TR had campaigned as soon as he found this expedient.

I did not attend the Progressive Party Convention in Chicago that made TR the official nominee for the presidency on the Progressive Party ticket. But it is interesting to note in the diary entry dated August 6 that when I returned to Oyster Bay after an absence, my mother reported that TR "told her just before he left for Chicago that although he had considered it an absolutely hopeless fight, it really looks now as if there were a possibility, but only the slightest possibility, of his being elected."

Four days later, on August 10, the diary reads that while Ethel and I were playing tennis, "TR and Archie appeared. The former looked younger by ten years than when I had last seen him and was in such wonderful spirits that he behaved like a boy. I have never known him to be gayer and more full of fun. When he first spied me he waved his racket in the air frantically, and when I tried to find out the time from him he grabbed me and beat me over the head with his racket and called out: 'You've got to play a set of tennis! You've got to play a set of tennis!' "

"When we got started [he and I playing against Ethel and Archie] he kept making fun of them and cracking jokes, and whenever a special shot of his fooled them he hopped across the court on one foot, singing and chortling." That evening we dined at Sagamore, and, according to the diary, he told us how he was "dumbfounded at the remarkable success that attended the Progressive Convention, and the spirit of religious fervor that seemed to have taken hold of the movement, and he considered it one of the triumphs of his life. No wonder that a man who received such a phenomenal demonstration of enthusiastic loyalty, carried to a pitch almost of religious frenzy, should feel happy."

After the meal TR, his sons Theodore, Jr. and Archie, and George Roosevelt and I adjourned to the porch at Sagamore and sat in rocking chairs as we discussed the progress of the campaign. The diary notes, after some slightly caustic comments of mine about the irrepressible urge of TR's son Ted to monopolize the conversation, that "George Roosevelt brought out one fine point: In the old days TR was the progressive leader of the conservatives, and now he was the conservative leader of the progressives. To which TR echoed: 'Yes, yes! That's it! I have to hold them in check all the time. I've got to restrain them.' "

On August 13 we had a family picnic at Jayne's Hill, about ten miles from Sagamore, to which TR, Archie, and I walked. The diary reads: "It was what he calls an 'old man's walk'—a rapid tramp across country, over fences and through fields, in a broiling sun. In the course of the walk he talked much about the political situation and he remarked, among other things, that the Progressive party was the first party in history to have a strictly sociological platform and added that, as such, it was of great importance. He emphasized that it was the end he was after as regards these issues and that he didn't give a rap under what guise they were brought about."

I also noted with interest that when I told him that Miss Louisa Lee Schuyler, an old friend of the family, had asked me how he "felt the pulse of" the country, his reply was: "I don't know the way the people *do* feel all over the country. I only know how they *ought* to feel." This answer reminds me of another remark of his which I heard him make—that one of the things that impressed him most as he looked back over his political experience was how almost inevitably the people of the country, once given time and a full presentation of all the facts in a political question at issue, would make a right decision. It was only when part of the basic information was withheld from them that they were inclined to be wrong.

On my last trip to Oyster Bay before Election Day I breakfasted at Sagamore and noted in the diary that while Cousin Edith and I were optimistic about the outcome, TR and Archie were not so confident.

As TR was pouring out his coffee he said he thought the chances were really only one out of four. I was surprised, and we had a little argument among us four, Cousin Edith and I against Archie and his father. When TR had eaten a heaping plate of liver and bacon, we adjourned to the library—he with another huge cup of coffee—and there we resumed the discussion. . . . Cousin Edith then started to read a few headlines from the *Times* which were particularly notable. These indicated that the Democrats were no longer certain and that New York was in doubt. . . . "Don't you think that's good news, Theodore?" she asked. [The diary continues:] He paused for a minute, always rocking his chair, and then grinning, suddenly exploded in a sort of amused reflective tone: "By George, you know, we've really got a chance!"

Subsequently he turned to an analysis of the probable election results: "TR offered Taft the chance of getting fifteen electoral votes. That was the biggest possible number, and there was even a chance that he would get none. [He actually got eight.] Among the possible Taft states he put Vermont, New Hampshire, Iowa, Wyoming and Idaho." (Taft carried only Vermont and Utah.) It is both interesting and characteristic that the final notation in the diary about the campaign is: "The very first thing he [TR] said when I saw him on Saturday after the election was: 'Well, Nick, it's been a bully fight! We've done perfectly wonderfully!' " The final returns showed that he had received just under 27.5 per cent of the popular vote to Taft's 23.2 per cent and that Wilson had just under 42 per cent. The balance was divided among splinter parties. Whether Taft would have beaten Wilson if TR had not run on the Bull Moose ticket is anybody's guess. Which is another way of saying that the commonly heard contention that TR was responsible for the election of Wilson is also hard to prove. What would have been the outcome if TR had been nominated by the Republicans?

10

PRAGMATIC REFORMER

TR's CRITICS, before and after 1912, characterized him as a "madman," a "revolutionary," a "subversive." And yet, if we start from the premise, which I believe to be sound, that the platform of the Progressive Party in 1912 embodied the full extent of his "radicalism," a reexamination of this document in the light of what has happened in the last half-century makes this radicalism seem surprisingly mild. The phrase with which he characterized the Progressive Party platform to Archie and me in the summer of 1912 is descriptive—"strictly sociological"—but as nearly all of its recommendations have since been incorporated into our political thinking as well as our laws it is hard to visualize the intensity of the bitterness that platform then aroused. I have before me a copy of the platform that he gave me on his return from the Progressive convention in Chicago—a document that today is of little interest to anyone other than a political antiquarian. I list its main points: direct primaries for the nomination of state and national officers, and, in particular, for candidates for the presidency; direct election of United States senators; bringing under effective national jurisdiction those problems which have expanded beyond reach of the individual states; effective legislation directed toward the prevention of industrial accidents, occupational diseases, and other similar risks of industry; the establishment of minimum safety and health standards in industry; prohibition of night work for women and establishment of an eight-hour day for women and young persons; the six-day week for all wage workers; the eight-hour day in continuous industries; full publicity as to wages, hours, and conditions of labor and industrial accidents; compensation for death by industrial accidents; a system of social insurance; the organization of the workers of the country into unions; national regulation of interstate corporations; the establishment of an administrative commission to supervise corporations engaged in interstate commerce; downward revision of the tariff; establishment of a nonpartisan scientific tariff commission; protection and conservation of the nation's natural resources, development of the Mississippi River and its tributaries, and the control of floods through water storage and levees; the opening up of the coal resources of Alaska; equal suffrage; the establishment of a department of labor; the creation of a national health service; extension of the powers of the interstate commerce commission to value the physical properties of railroads; the construction of national highways; imposition of a graduated inheritance tax; ratification of the amendment providing for a federal income tax; the building of two battleships a year; provision of pensions for American soldiers and sailors and their widows and children; the establishment of a parcel post system; the substitution of a civil service for the spoils system; and, finally, two propositions restraining the powers of the courts.

[I quote in full from the platform] (1) That when an act, passed under the police power of the state, is held unconstitutional under the state constitution, by the courts, the people, after an ample interval for deliberation, shall have an opportunity to vote on the question whether they desire the act to become a law, notwithstanding such decision. (2) That every decision of the highest appellate court of a state declaring an act of the legislature unconstitutional on the ground of its violation of the Federal constitution shall be subject to the same review by the Supreme Court of the United States as is now accorded to decisions sustaining such legislation.

Most of the points made in this platform had already been advocated by TR in his speech on "The New Nationalism," which he made at Osawotamie, Kansas, in 1910. In 1914, two years after he had been defeated on the Progressive Party platform he wrote to Raymond Robins that "My Osawotamie speech represented my deepest convictions and instead of going back from it I feel we must steadily go forward from it."[1] In the same letter he stated: "I am in every fibre of my body a radical." While I think this is an exaggeration, it is a characteristic expression of his own realization that he saw clearly the nature not only of the economic changes that had come about during the half-century since the Civil War, but also the changes in our political structure that had to be made in order effectively to cope with new economic and social conditions. In applying to him the term *pragmatic reformer* I suggest that he had learned from personal observation and experience and that the reforms which he advocated were for the most part practical rather than theoretical. His keen intelligence enabled him to learn quickly, and, as I have stressed before, once he reached a decision he was prompt in acting upon it. Merely to note or to call attention to injustice or evil or corruption was not enough for him. He put his mind on how it could be eliminated or mitigated and then did something about it.

An excellent early illustration of this followed his appointment in 1883 as one of a committee of three members of the New York State Assembly to investigate conditions in tenement houses in New York City in connection with a bill introduced at the request of the Cigar Makers Union to prohibit the manufacture of cigars in tenement houses. By upbringing and background TR was inclined at the time to be against government interference in such matters. But when he went with Samuel Gompers to inspect tenements in which cigar-making was being carried on he found conditions so shocking from a health and social point of view that he became an ardent champion of the proposed reform and urged the governor to sign the bill, which he did.[2] A year later the bill was declared unconstitutional by the New York Court of Appeals on the ground that it was an assault on the hallowed influences of the home. On which TR commented in his autobiography thirty years later that "it was this case which first waked me to a dim and partial understanding of the fact that the courts were not necessarily the best judges of what should be done to better social and industrial conditions."[3] This decision, as TR pointed out, blocked tenement house reform legislation in New York for decades—and, incidentally, became influential in determining TR to seek means for making it possible to reverse court decisions that so patently blocked needed legislative acts.

The details of TR's early development as a practical reformer have been ably set forth by such biographers as Carleton Putnam and W. H. Harbaugh. As I look back over TR's career I have been increasingly impressed with the far-reaching consequences of his work in this field. I was therefore interested to find a diary entry dated January 28, 1912, saying that when I went up to Sagamore after lunch on that day, I found the French ambassador, M. Jules Jusserand there. He and TR were engaged in a discussion about the latter's main achievement in the White House. M. Jusserand said "that he considered TR's greatest work to have been the stimulus of public opinion to investigation and to a demand for the square deal." That TR was fully conscious of the importance of this work is evident from the fact that in his autobiography he inserted in an appendix an estimate by a man whose dislike of TR was notorious—Senator Robert M. LaFollette—which stated that TR had "left impressed on the American mind the one great truth of economic justice couched in the pithy and stinging phrase, 'the square deal.' " LaFollette added that the task of "making reform respectable in a commercialized world and of giving the nation a slogan in a phrase is greater than the man who performed it is likely to think."[4]

The significance of TR's work as a political and social reformer a half century ago lies in the fact that the growth of vast corporate structures in the decades after the Civil War had led to widespread political corruption and had facilitated the concentration of enormous financial and political powers in the hands of a relatively small number of businessmen. The relationship between business and politics by that time may be described as a partnership entered into for profit with mutually tolerant cynicism. Big business fattened on special privileges that derived from political compliance. Business leaders were ready to pay—and to pay well—for franchises and other governmental favors. But they expected government acquiesence—not interference or regulation. Most local and state politicians were glad to oblige—for values promised. As H. U. Faulkner put it in his volume *The Quest for Social Justice*, the party machinery at the state and municipal levels was at this time "at the beck and call of railroad and corporation interests which understood all too well the means whereby legislators were made their pliant tools."[5]

TR's experience in the White House made it plain to him that the growth of great corporate structures since the Civil War had created conditions that called for controls that transcended state lines—controls that the states by themselves could not effectively impose. It was to create machinery to regulate big business operations in two or more states that the powers of the federal government had to be enlarged.

As the reforms for which he fought could only be put over by political action and as most of the professional politicians, backed by business interests, favored the status quo, TR took special pains to arouse public support for desired reforms. With the dramatic agility of a skilled publicist and the ardor of a revivalist he made it a point in countless speeches and messages to dramatize himself as on the side of the angels—and usually their leader—and to brand his foes as in league with the devil. Because many big businessmen were as vulnerable ethically as they were successful financially, it was easy for him to lump them together as "malefactors of great wealth" and to pillory them as responsible for the corruption of state and local governments. A good example of the kind of invective that he effectively used is to be found in a letter that he addressed to Attorney-General Charles J. Bonaparte, in which he referred to "the representatives of predatory wealth, of wealth accumulated on a giant scale by iniquity, by wrong-doing in many forms, by plain swindling, by oppressing wage workers, by manipulating securities, by unfair and unwholesome competition and by stock-jobbing—in short, by conduct abhorrent to every man of ordinarily decent conscience"—and he went on to say that these men had "made it evident that they are banded together to work for reaction, to endeavor to overthrow all who honestly administer the law, and to secure a return to the days when every unscrupulous wrongdoer could do what he wished unchecked provided he had enough money."[6]

In the process of denouncing wicked business tycoons TR dramatized the crookedness of the political leaders who abetted them. He thus directed public attention against abuses in the political as well as in the business world. The voters, sensing his sincerity hailed his crusading spirit and delighted in his picturesque and pugnacious language. Even the newspapers that most hated him gave space to what he said, as he was always "good copy"—colorful and interesting, whether in the role of hero or villain, and never dull except to the dull and stuffy.

While TR owed much of his success as a reformer to his skill in mobilizing public opinion his effectiveness in the final analysis was largely determined by his political agility. As has been made clear in preceding chapters he was a shrewd politician. He made mistakes, of course, and on occasions worked himself into situations that defeated his objectives. But he knew that no one could be effective in American politics by trying to move single-handed in a given direction and that it was not only expedient but right that there should be compromises in the implementation of objectives under our form of government. TR's experience in various political offices had taught him that even a strong and willful executive cannot have his way without the cooperation of the legislative branch of the government. In his autobiography he speaks of having, early in his days in the assembly "learned the invaluable lesson that in the practical activities of life no man can render the highest service unless he can act in combination with his fellows, which means a certain amount of give and take between him and them."[7] In the presidency TR consistently made it a point to work with the Republican leaders in both houses of Congress, without whose approval and help needed legislation would be unobtainable. Only in the sphere of the executive department did he ignore congressional leaders, as, under the Constitution, he was entitled to do. In fact, he was notably touchy about any infringement on the prerogatives of the executive by members of either house of Congress.

Biographers and historians have speculated about TR's hopes and ambitions for 1916. I saw him repeatedly after my return from Europe in the spring of that year and at his suggestion went to see General Leonard Wood, who was then in command at Governor's Island, as to Wood's possible availability as a candidate—a suggestion that TR later made to Nicholas Murray Butler at the Republican National Convention. On Election Day in 1916 I drove TR to the polling booth in Oyster Bay, where both of us voted for "that whiskered Wilson," Charles Evans Hughes. If TR wanted the office "oh so badly!" (the words are those of one of the more studious biographers of TR) he managed successfully to hide his ambition from his family and close relatives.

That TR had little enthusiasm for Hughes as a possible president and that he was increasingly scathing about Wilson was clear to all who knew him. Surely there were times when he felt that he, TR, would have handled a particular crisis more effectively than did Wilson. I have a number of letters from him ending with the refrain: "How I would like to have been president to handle our foreign policy as regards Mexico, and as regards this European war!" But neither at the time nor in retrospect did these asides suggest to me that he was "power hungry." Rather did they seem to be the natural reactions of an expert watching an inexperienced man following a course that the expert foresaw was self-defeating and would be paid for in human lives.

Down into the first week in November, 1916, Woodrow Wilson encouraged his supporters to center their campaign for his reelection on the slogan: "He kept us out of war!" Within five weeks of Wilson's second inaugural Wilson declared that a state of war existed between the United States and Germany. Twenty-three months had passed since the German Embassy in Washington had published an advertisement in the New York papers warning Americans against sailing for Europe on the *Lusitania*—which brought from TR a letter to J. C. O'Laughlin dated May 6, 1915, (the day before the *Lusitania* was torpedoed) saying that if he were President and "if any of our people were sunk on the *Lusitania*, I would confiscate all the German interned ships."[8] The day after the sinking he wrote to me, saying: "If I were President now I would take the most emphatic action about the German conduct in sinking the *Lusitania*. I regard this as sheer murder, and the whole German attitude in this war has been a return, quite a long distance, toward the attitude of those heroes of the amiable Kaiser, the Huns. There is only one way to meet people who adopt such an attitude, and that is, to make them suffer for maintaining it."

Is there any wonder that the realist who had been President looked with such bitterness on the so-called idealist in the White House who for twenty-three months had delayed facing and preparing for the inevitable?

11

CAMPING COMPANION

SHORTLY AFTER THE 1912 ELECTION TR, Archie, Quentin, and I discussed the possibility of going on a hunting trip the following summer on the North Rim of the Grand Canyon. As plans evolved it was agreed that I would take two horses which Archie had left at the Evans ranch in Mesa, Arizona, as well as horses of my own and go from Mesa to Kanab, Utah, by way of Lee's Ferry. In those days Lee's Ferry was the only place in Arizona where it was possible to cross the Grand Canyon with horses and teams. In Kanab I was to arrange for a pack outfit for us to use to hunt mountain lions when we joined "Uncle" Jim Owens, the government hunter stationed at Bright Angel Camp on the North Rim. The Kaibab Plateau or Buckskin Mountain, as the North Rim of the Grand Canyon then was locally known, had been made into a national monument by TR during the last year of his presidency.

I reached Kanab early in June, 1913, with Archie's and my horses, and discussed with a firm of camping outfitters the details of the kind of outfit that we would need. I have letters from TR setting forth what he thought would be desirable. The earliest, dated March 26, 1913, suggested that I get a first-class guide and boss of the outfit who knew the country thoroughly and consult him as to what we would need.

There should be two or three men with it, one cook and two packers [he wrote me]. There must be a horse for each member of the party, including Archie's two horses. Consult the guide as to the number of the pack animals, taking his advice as to whether they should be mules or horses. I should think that we would need twelve. Also consult with the guide about the more common foods: That is, the amount of flour, sugar, salt and bacon. We will bring about fifteen pounds of coffee, and some tea in addition. I suggest an ample supply of Frejoles [Mexican dried beans, now usually spelled *frijoles*], some jerky [smoked venison], dried fruit (not prunes) thirty cans of sardines and a supply of Borden's condensed milk. Ask the guide about the tentage. I think the lightest and smallest tents, merely to be used for emergencies in wet weather would be the best. For cooking outfit also consult the guide and use your own discretion. I suggest, however, two medium Dutch ovens instead of one large one. Two or more frying pans, one big coffee pot, one small tea pot, three or four cooking pots, knives, forks, spoons, cups and saucers for each man. Four big canteens as well as, possibly to go on the pack horses, four largest sized saddle canteens. Plenty of matches and two light axes.

Ten days later TR wrote again "about a waterproof silk sleeping tent. I don't want a tent to stand up in. Only one to sleep in if it rains, because, unlike you young people, I am rheumatic. I don't want to put up the tent at all unless it rains." He added, apparently in reply to a letter of mine: "I agree with you that the smaller our outfit is, the better. . . . I have no doubt a pack horse to each man would be ample." On May 24 he wrote: "We will bring our bedding and clothes and the saddles. As I have already explained, I would like you to get both Quentin and me bridles. My outfit won't weigh much. There is an ordinary blanket sleeping bag and a small war sack with one complete change in it. That is about all. I will order the biggest canteen I can for myself personally, but I believe it would be a good thing for you to order an extra one for me. I won't try to bring any food unless perhaps a little chocolate."

I concluded the arrangements with the outfitters in Kanab.

A copy of the agreement with the Grand Canyon Transportation Company dated June 23, 1913, which I have in my files, refers to furnishing us a guide and a cook, both mounted, and four first-rate saddle horses with pack outfit complete, together with food for the outfit for the period July 15 to August 2 inclusive. It was agreed that the outfit should meet us early on the morning of July 15 at the bottom of the Grand Canyon, on the north side of the Colorado River, where a hand-winch operated, suspended cable car had been installed a number of years previously.

On July 6 I crossed over the river from north to south in this cable car to spend a few days in Flagstaff before meeting TR and Archie and Quentin on the Santa Fe Railway's "California Limited" as it passed through that town. We reached Grand Canyon the evening of July 12. During the next two days TR and Quentin did some preliminary riding there, and early on the morning of the fifteenth we started down Bright Angel Trail, accompanied by Jesse Cummins, a ranchhand from Mesa whom Archie and I had known and liked and who was to be with us on the trip.

We had an easy ride down into the Canyon on mules rented from El Tovar Hotel. The diary reads: "By the time we reached the river there was a booming thunderstorm in progress. . . . TR and the four of us piled into the caged cable car which was to take us across the river and signalled to the man on the other side to start hauling us over. The cage went very slowly and irregularly, stopping for a minute at a time. [When I had crossed from north to south a week previously the trip had been continuous and relatively rapid.] I couldn't imagine what was wrong. The thunder boomed and re-echoed almost steadily as we hung fifty feet above the river." For several minutes the car did not move at all. TR, even though he gloried in the unusual experience, wanted to know why we were left there in the lurch. Slowly the car began to move again, and as we reached the north

Theodore Roosevelt in his study at Sagamore Hill, 1905

TR's sister "Bamie," Anna Cowles

Edith Kermit Roosevelt, TR's second wife. From a drawing by John Singer Sargent, 1921.

Right: TR and Edith. *Below:* TR's first wife, Alice Lee, and his sisters, Corinne and "Bamie."

Sagamore Hill, TR's summer home on Long Island. *Below:* The Trophy Room at Sagamore Hill.

The Roosevelt cousins in an obstacle race. TR holds the watch.

The sixteen Roosevelt cousins on the lawn at Sagamore Hill. The author is second from left. *Below:* The TR family, 1903. Ethel, TR, TR, Jr., Archie, Alice, Kermit, Edith, and Quentin.

A family soccer game at Sagamore Hill. *Below:* Archie Roosevelt, left, and Nicholas, the author, at Sagamore Hill.

The start of a family ride, Sagamore Hill, 1903. Archie, Kermit, TR, Edith, and Quentin. *Below:* The Roosevelt cousins on the lawn at Sagamore Hill, with the author third from left.

Above: Mrs. TR and a friend in the phaeton driven by Julius on Long Island. *Right:* Mrs. TR and TR, Jr., 1903.

Left: TR and family at a campfire on the dunes, 1905. *Below:* TR chopping wood, 1912.

TR leading a family hike, 1904. *Below:* TR on the shore of Oyster Bay, 1905.

Left: TR reading in a cabin, 1905. *Below:* The three TR's.

Above: TR speaks to the crowd outside Convention Hall, 1912. *Right:* TR arrives in New York to rally the Progressive Party, 1912.

TR and Sir George Otto Trevelyan, June 4th, 1910

TR and his granddaughter, Edith Roosevelt Derby, 1918

TR speaks to the soldiers at an Officer's Training Camp in Plattsburg, N. Y., 1915

TR and General Wood, at Plattsburg, 1915

side I was surprised to see, instead of the guide whom I had engaged, an old man, exhausted from the effort of cranking our cage across the broad river. He was as surprised as we were, but —again I quote from the diary—"when he recognized TR he exclaimed 'I've always been a Democrat, Colonel, but I'm an admirer of Roosevelt and I want to shake you by the hand.'" He turned out to be the foreman of the Bar Z ranch, which ran cattle and buffalo on the North Rim. When we asked him if he had seen our outfit he answered: "No," and asked us if we had seen Mr. Stevenson, the owner of the Bar Z ranch, when we were at the El Tovar Hotel on the south side of the Canyon. In a few minutes we heard shots fired on the other side of the river and realized that they must come from the Stevenson party. Archie, Quentin, and I took over the tough job of winching the hanging cable car across the river and back, bearing three officials of the Bar Z ranch. These were delighted to meet TR, and had spare horses which TR and Quentin could ride up the 7,000-foot climb to the North Rim.

The incident was typical of the kind of luck that seemed to follow TR everywhere. We had reached the bottom of the Grand Canyon, to find no trace of the outfit which was to meet us there, and yet, within a few minutes of our arrival at this cable crossing, in a remote wilderness, that was used scarcely a dozen times a year another outfit arrived, able to furnish us the food and transportation that we needed.

On the advice of Mr. Stevenson it was decided that we would spend the night at the bottom of the canyon and start the climb before dawn. TR enjoyed himself immensely, untroubled by the failure of our outfit to appear on time, and the discomfort thereby entailed. Since he and Stevenson found it hard to get to sleep because of the continual roar of the river they talked for hours of ranching, hunting, and our relations with Mexico.

The diary reads:

Mansfield [the foreman of the Bar Z] got us up at 1.30 a.m. and after a breakfast of cornmeal mush and canned chicken, Archie, Jesse Cummins and I set forth on foot at 2.45 a.m. on a cloudy night. TR and Quentin were mounted, and were to give us a head start. The first five miles of the trail was up a box canyon with perpendicular walls rising hundreds of feet. We had to walk in the creek bed, and we had to ford the creek more than a hundred times. The small patches of sky which we could see gave a ghostly light, and made the canyon walls look taller. . . . We slid and stumbled and waded knee deep over slippery rocks in the creek, falling every now and then, and constantly losing the trail in the water, and striking bad crossings. In a few hours the horses caught up with us, and by daylight we rose out of the box to start upon three hours fairly easy climbing up a trail along Bright Angel Creek.

When we reached the top we found our outfit from Kanab preparing to start down to meet us. It turned out that they had thought that this day was the fourteenth of July, whereas in fact it was the sixteenth, and had planned to meet us early the next morning at the bottom of the canyon, unaware that they were two days late. As a result of this misunderstanding TR decided that we would get along without them and that we would accept the Bar Z's offer to lend us riding horses and would use as pack animals the two pack horses that I had brought, as well as a mule and two donkeys which belonged to Uncle Jim Owens. In addition to Jesse Cummins we arranged to pick up a prospector whom I had met on the Rim known as "Joe" (with no further identification as he was apparently "wanted" by the law) to help with the horses and packing. TR was amused and pleased with our odd collection of pack animals and was delighted to hear from Uncle Jim that wherever possible we would "live off the land," eating such fare as mountain lion meat and the flesh of wild horses.

As Uncle Jim knew the area well, we left it to him to decide where we should camp and hunt. Uncle Jim had back of him a long life on the frontier. While he never disclosed his age, we figured that he must be about seventy. He told me that he had worked on the Goodnight ranch in the Texas panhandle after the Civil War, and that it was he who had introduced the practice of moving cattle in the cool of the night instead of in the heat of the day when they were being driven long distances to the rail head in Kansas to be shipped to the stockyards. Not only was this easier on the stock, but they lost less weight through evaporation. A Texan by birth and almost illiterate, Uncle Jim had a diffident and sad air, but there was iron in his soul. He had the manners of a gentleman and was free from spite and malice. In the weeks that I spent with him before and after the arrival of TR I never heard an unkind or an unclean word from him or a discourteous one. He had a simple philosophy of conduct—that kindness was of utmost importance and should govern at all times.

Uncle Jim was a crack shot with a revolver as well as with a rifle, as may be deduced from a note in my diary that I had "seen him fire three shots at a jack rabbit, removing both ears and then cracking the top of the skull, so as in no way to mangle the animal for cooking." The government had made him game warden with the job of killing predators such as cougars, wildcats, bears, and coyotes. So as to provide adequate food for his dogs, he was also authorized to shoot wild horses, of which there were many on the North Rim.

Of Uncle Jim's five dogs his pet was Pot, an ochre-colored, red-spotted hound, which Uncle Jim had raised on canned milk when its mother died shortly after its birth. Jim kept Pot as a pup in a sock, and when he went hunting, he put Pot in a nosebag and slung the nosebag on his saddle. Thus Pot from his earliest days was accustomed to the sounds of hunting. As he grew up under the guidance of Uncle Jim's best-trained older dogs, Pot became an expert hunter and took part in the tracking and killing of more than one hundred and fifty cougars.

Uncle Jim was of the breed of Daniel Boone—at home in

the forest, wise in the ways of the wilderness, a hunter by profession and need, self-reliant, resourceful, tough, almost indestructible. Our other main assistant, Jesse Cummins, belonged to a later school of pioneers. More at home in a mining camp than in the woods, Jesse had prospected Superstition Mountain in the Salt River Valley for years without success, but was still sure that he would soon strike it rich. He could shoe a horse, mend a saddle, shoot, cook, or do anything that was useful in the wilderness, but his luck was brightest in his dreams. Uncle Jim spoke little. Jesse was full of cheerful talk, humorous and shrewd.

It was TR's hope that Archie, Quentin, and I would each get a lion. After we had done this he would try for one. We were to toss for first shot. I won the first toss. At Uncle Jim's suggestion he followed the dogs closely on his mule, with a nosebag full of small stones—"rocks," he called them—to throw at the dogs when they took off on a wrong scent. Jim wanted the shooter of the day to follow close behind him and the rest to trail along afterward. On this first day we rode along the rim of the canyon for an hour or more, when (I quote from the diary)

> the five hounds who had been nosing about, shot off, and we galloped after them, dodging trees as best we could. I was behind Uncle Jim. As we crossed a gulch I saw a brown form streak through the quaking aspens towards the canyon rim. Uncle Jim said it was the lion—it had backtracked the dogs. For a while we followed the dogs on the trail of the mate but Uncle Jim soon called them back to the fresher trail, and they followed it with a roar. They tore down a steep side-canyon and we could hear them rushing to the ledge below. Then we heard them barking and knew that they had treed the lion. Tying our horses above the rim we scrambled down into the Grand Canyon after Uncle Jim. It was like climbing down the roof of a house. On the way down we passed TR and raced up the side of the ledge where the lion lay crouched high in a pine tree. Our noise scared him. He jumped from one tree to another. I shot at him, but

being a hundred yards away and a poor shot, I missed. As he crouched across two branches, one hind leg hanging down, scarcely twenty feet above the side of the canyon, he lashed his tail and snarled at the dogs.

In due time I had a chance for a good aim and killed him with the first shot. Uncle Jim and Archie and I caught the lion to keep him from sliding over the edge of the canyon. He was a big male with a fine pelt.

TR came up as we grabbed the lion and—again I quote from the diary—"apologized for being so slow, explaining that he was an old man. His 'so slow' was only 20 feet behind us, and his 'old man' talk was misleading. He still has the energy of a boy and is handicapped only by his weight. He was as delighted as if he had made the kill himself, and talked a blue streak." Later in the diary I referred to TR "chanting a song of victory." It appears that from his early hunting days onward he went through a sort of ritual of delight when he or those hunting with him shot successfully.

On rereading the articles that he wrote for *Outlook* about this trip I am struck with the breadth of his interests and the meticulousness with which he detailed the birds and other animals that we encountered and described the country through which we rode and hunted. As a camping companion no one could have been pleasanter than TR. Cheerful, self-sufficient, and undemanding, he always had a word of praise for the cook and of thanks to the wranglers when, after long searches for the hobbled horses that had wandered off into the woods, they finally brought them into camp. While he was glad to have us help in saddling his horse and in loading and cinching the pack animals, he helped in gathering firewood when we made camp and took his share of camp chores. He always laid out his own bedding roll and did it up when we moved camp. He washed his own laundry, and every afternoon when we came back to camp from the hunt he got a cup of hot water from the cook and shaved and bathed.

At all times he was scrupulously clean—which I see from a letter he wrote my mother, was not always the case with the younger generation inasmuch as, after commending Archie's and my ability to adapt ourselves to the roughest conditions, he added: "They are not exactly pretty now, by the way, for they are the very dirtiest objects you have ever seen." When the evening meal was over TR would settle down in a comfortable spot, preferably with his back against a tree, and spin yarns about hunting trips elsewhere. Never was he out of sorts or grumpy. Never did he say an unkind word to any of us.

On August 1 we ended the first lap of our trip, leaving the cool wooded Kaibab Plateau for House Rock Valley—a descent of several thousand feet into desert country, barren, hot, and dry. As we neared an old stone house and corral in the valley that Uncle Jim occasionally used in winter when tending the small herd of buffalo of which he was part owner, a fierce sandstorm struck us, and we crouched in the lee of the stone house until it passed and then resumed our ride across the desert toward the wall of the Vermillion Cliffs, which marked the eastern edge of the House Rock Valley. This road—little more than a trail—turned south at the foot of the cliffs. As we stopped to rest the horses in the shade of a gigantic boulder TR quoted the verse from the Book of Isaiah about the comfort of "the shadow of a great rock in a weary land."

The next day we reached the irrigated green pastures of Lee's Ferry—then owned by the Bar Z ranch—and were welcomed by the Bar Z representative and given fresh fruit and vegetables by his wife. We were glad to learn from him that the outfit that Don Lorenzo Hubbell, owner of the Indian trading post at Ganado, was to furnish us to make the overland journey to Kayenta and the Hopi Villages had arrived two days ahead of time and was camped on the other side of the river. Archie and I crossed the Colorado on the ferry and found, as I was sure would be the case, that Don Lorenzo had provided well for our needs. He had sent a wagon and mules, with plenty of food, water, and grain. The driver was a Mexican, Francisco Marquez, and the cook was a Navajo by the name of Loco, whom I had known when I had been at Ganado two years previously. These two brought one of the wagons across the ferry and established a comfortable camp for us near the Bar Z's corral. The next afternoon we moved everything, including Archie's and my horses and all our equipment, to the south side of the river and camped there overnight so that we could make an early start the next morning on the long trek skirting the Painted Desert to Tuba City. From Tuba we went to Marsh Pass and thence to the Wetherell's trading post at Kayenta—a total distance of about one hundred and fifty miles from Lee's Ferry, most of it over sandy roads with little feed for the stock and very little water.

Kayenta then was in the heart of the Navajo country, and the Navajos still retained a pastoral culture in which weaving and the making of silver and turquoise jewelry had been well developed. The Wetherells were not only traders but students of Navajo myths and customs and patrons of Navajo art. Mrs. Wetherell, in particular, had made a study of their myths and and sand paintings and collected examples of jewelry and weaving. She spoke the language well and had many friends among Navajo medicine men and among the women of the tribe. She and TR spent interested hours in discussing Indian mythology and the problem of how to educate Navajo children for more active participation in American life without undercutting their own cultural heritage—a subject to which TR devoted a part of his article in *Outlook* entitled "Across the Navajo Desert."

On August 10, under Mr. Wetherell's guidance, we started for the Rainbow Natural Bridge, which had been first seen by white men only four years previously. Ours was the eleventh party that Wetherell, who had accompanied all our predecessors, had taken in. The party immediately preceding ours was headed by the subsequently well-known writer of westerns, Zane Grey.

The trail that went by Marsh Pass through Bubbling Spring Canyon and around the north slope of Navajo Mountain was in those days rough on riders and actually dangerous in places for horses. We came on the first of these (I quote from the diary)

> when we rode into a narrow, shallow rock-walled canyon terminating in an abrupt rocky dome. Here we led the loose horses and proceeded to clamber up this red sandstone dome on foot. I would have thought that it was impossible to get a horse over it. But they managed to stick, and we rounded the top of the dome to find before us a number of whaleback dunes made of sand rock. Around the side of the first of these we went, the horses clinging on by grace of a six inch ledge on the rounded side of the dome. Had they slipped they would have slid fifty feet into a canyon below, without a chance of being saved. Over a level sand rock whaleback we climbed up another dome, and then came to where it sloped down for a hundred feet, at a curve so great that we could only keep our footing because it was rough sandstone. . . . Fortunately none of the horses slipped—though Mr. Wetherell has lost several here.

This was merely the introduction. The diary reads:

> At last we came to what seemed like a crack in the rock. It was about four feet wide and filled with boulders. It dropped downwards for several hundred yards at a rideable slope, and down it we led our horses. . . . When we were 200 feet below the top of the walls we came to two enormous boulders. The pack animals disappeared between them, and we heard a terrific crashing and sliding of stones. One by one the other horses went through and when my turn came I beheld a drop of fifty feet almost perpendicular over which a rotten trail zigzagged. The horses before me were slipping and sliding and mine brought rocks on my heels.

TR, in his *Outlook* article, went on to explain that "the last four miles were the worst of all for the horses. They led along to the bottom of the Bridge canyon. It was covered with a torrent-strewn mass of smooth rocks, from pebbles to boulders of a ton's weight. It was a marvel that the horses got down without breaking their legs; and the poor beasts were nearly worn out."

The diary continues: "Rounding a little projection in the canyon we saw before us an enormous red sandstone arch shaped like a rainbow, stretching from one side of the canyon across to the other. It was difficult to grasp the enormous size of it until we came beneath it. Then TR, Archie, Quentin and I lay down on our backs and looked up at it as the sun was going behind the cliff walls. In this manner we could see the enormous beam of the arch, as high above us as the vault of a cathedral." As there were several pools under the arch, TR appropriated one, and we three boys went to another in which we could swim. When we were cooled and refreshed we found that Wetherell and Jesse Cummins had built a fire directly under the north span of the arch, and there we ate our supper; and as the last light was fading in the west the full moon rose over the canyon wall and lighted up the arch. As TR rightly noted, it is surely one of the wonders of the world—and for a half-century after our visit thousands of hardy hikers have marveled at its beauty. But it is now (1967) destined for destruction—or at least serious damage —in the name of progress and utility because unimaginative engineers commissioned to impound the waters of the Colorado for hydroelectric purposes have planned to flood the bridge canyon to the foot of the natural bridge.

On our return to Kayenta from the Rainbow Natural Bridge the next day we decided to cut across the Black Mesa to the Hopi villages with a pack train instead of accompanying the wagon by way of Tuba City. We had as guides and assistants two cheerful young Navajos. It was a two-day ride to Walpi, where Lorenzo Hubbell was waiting for us. He told us of the arrangements that he had made for us to see the snake-washing ceremonies before the snake dance.

Few whites have ever seen this, but thanks to Mr. Hubbell's influence and to the fact that TR had been President, we were invited to see it. The ceremony was to start at noon in the underground kiva of the snake clan. When we arrived there no one seemed to be expecting us. The diary reads:

At last an old priest came out wearing a red calico shirt and whispered a word to Mr. Hubbell. "All right, boys, come on," said the Honorable Lorenzo, and we all of us got up and went to the entrance of the snake kiva. The priest went in first and Hubbell then ushered in TR and Abbott [the Indian agent]. We three boys went in last, and as I took off my hat and started down into the kiva I felt pretty thoroughly excited. But the moment I got down all my excitement left me and to my surprise I lost all sense of loathing when I stood on the dais with some hundred snakes—more than half rattlers—within five feet of me. To look at them piled against the back of the kiva, slowly creeping about and crawling towards us gave me a sense of the utmost security.

Most of the priests got up as we came in. They were all clad in breach-clouts and were unpainted. The kiva, better lighted than I expected as it had a tiny window at the other end, was a room about 12 by 22 feet, with an 8-foot ceiling. At the western end was a stone bench, in the center of which was a square hole. On the walls were hung the ceremonial robes and a few masks. In front of the bench was an altar, consisting of a sandpainting representing a coyote with four snakes about it. Rainbows ran about the whole thing and formed a square border. The colors were red, white, yellow and green. There may have been more but I was in a poor position to see well. This painting was surrounded by a stockade of black thunder-sticks with feathers on them.

The ladder, which served as entrance, landed upon a sort of dais which was raised about eight inches above the rest of the kiva. It was on this dais that the snakes were crawling, and that, for a while, we stood. They were coiled and twined in piles, as near the wall as possible, all slowly twisting and moving. Whenever one slowly wound out towards us a priest gently brushed it back with eagle feathers.

The priests then squatted down in their nakedness, five against the north wall. Two stood with feathers by the altar and two by the snakes. One kept guard at the top on the outside. The rest were grouped indiscriminately, facing the five on the north wall. We whites, with a man whom TR said was the oldest living snake priest, were placed against the south wall. TR, Hubbell and Abbott, stood against it, and I knelt down in front of TR with the backs of the heads of the squatting priests between me and the five priests facing us. In front of one powerful priest was a big bowl filled with a dirty liquid. This bowl covered a painting of white sand—apparently geometrical.

After considerable whispering a ceremonial pipe was passed and the chief blew smoke into the bowl and sprinkled sacred meal into it. Then, after some hesitation, they grew quiet, and the chief spoke a prayer. Every few words the rest joined in with a word that seemed to correspond to our "amen." They then took their rattles and feathered sticks in hand and started very quietly shaking the rattles in imitation of the wind slowly rising. There was a fixed rhythm to this, and when it grew louder, the priests began a low chanting. To my inexperienced ear it seemed much like that in the antelope dance. The singing slowly grew louder, and at a signal from the chief, the two priests on the dais stepped back and each picked up two big rattlers. With perfect unconcern they handed them to the priests near the bowl, who held them a foot or more from their heads, and shook them up and down with the same motion as with the rattles. When several priests held snakes there was suddenly an infernal screeching from all the priests—truly a hellish noise—and they frantically dipped the snakes in the bowl and hurled them at the altar across the kiva. With perfect unconcern the singing was resumed while more snakes were handed out. Then with a suddenness which made me jump, there came again this fiendish screeching, and the snakes were immersed in the bowl and with howls flung at the altar. A more thrilling and hair-raising sight I have never seen, and I shall ever retain vividly the picture of these squatting naked savages chanting like monks, suddenly giving vent to these terrific screeches and flinging the snakes with all their force at the altar.

This was continued until all the snakes had been washed, and every time that they were dipped and hurled at the altar there was the same thrill as the priests screeched at the top of their lungs. The painting at the altar was soon destroyed, and at the opposite end to the dais the mass of snakes were moving around in a much more lively fashion. Some tried to crawl up the wall. Many persisted in crawling into the hole in the bench. This kept the two priests busy holding them away from our end, and generally quieting them. The priests continually reached in and emptied out the hole in the stone bench.

Throughout the ceremony the priests handled the snakes with the utmost indifference. They grabbed them only when necessary, but then paid little heed as to how far from the heads they grabbed. Most of the herding of the snakes was done with feathers with which they stroked them.

When the last snakes had been bathed the chanting subsided and the rattling continued, growing softer until it died away like the wind after a thunderstorm. For a few seconds there was absolute silence. Then once more the chief prayed and once more the rest joined in with their amen. When this was finished the chief priest said somthing to us and, walking over to the bowl, took a handful of sacred meal. He then stood over the altar, and in a low voice delivered a prayer as he sprinkled the meal over the snakes. Some of them crawled between his legs, which in no way seemed to bother him. The chief priest sprinkled sacred meal into the bowl, east, west, north, south, northeast and southwest, and in the center. Twice he blew smoke into it, and after a pause took a sack of sand which he scattered on the wet places on the floor. He then scraped it all up and moving the bowl to one side, scraped up the painting it had rested upon. This sand he put in the bowl and then carried it up out of the kiva.

After a few moments of silence they let us know that the ceremony was over, and we started on a round of thanks and good-bye.

"Tell them," said TR, "that as the former head of Washington, as the President, I thank the people of Walpi for the courtesy that they have shown me. Tell them that as a reward, if they ever have any trouble, to come to me, and I shall do everything in my power for them."

To this they grunted in a pleased fashion. Then the interpreter asked:

"What is your name?"

"President Roosevelt—Roosevelt—Washington."

Interpreter: "They ask for you to send them shells" (pointing to their bracelets).

TR: "Tell them I shall send them a sack full—two sacks full!"

And they then came up and shook hands with all of us, some using the Navajo greeting "Yahtay!" some the Hopi: "Lolomai!" and some "Good-bye!"

We then returned to the daylight again.

That afternoon the snake dance was held in the plaza, and shortly after it was over we were driven to Ganado in Mr. Hubbell's new Ford cars and spent the night and part of the next day at his trading post, enjoying his warm hospitality. The next morning he sent us to Gallup in time to board the California Limited for Chicago, where we caught the Pennsylvania Limited to New York. It had been an absorbing and varied summer—the last that TR spent in the vigor of full health, as he left that autumn for his Brazilian adventure from which he returned with recurrent fevers and other ailments, although still unimpaired in vigor of mind. His immense vitality kept him going for another four years—and they were years of great achievement. But the machine was running down and thereafter needed constant attention and repairs.

12

PROPHET OF CONSERVATION

DURING THE SUMMER of 1913 in Arizona, TR told us about his problems as President when he sought to set aside parts of the public domain as national forests or national monuments. I remember his saying that whenever he proposed to create a new national forest or monument three groups of lobbyists ganged up on Congress in hopes of blocking him—the lumber interests, the mining interests, and the grazing interests. They were usually abetted by the western railroads, which had received large grants in land in post-Civil War days. Inasmuch as most of these lands were in alternate sections, checkerboarded with public lands to a depth of six miles on each side of the railroad right-of-way, the railroads resisted on general principles any restrictions on the exploitation of the country's natural resources on public lands lest these might jeopardize future large-scale extractive operations. These pressure groups, whose influence on local and national politicians was as sordid as it was effective, joined in opposing the conservation of the nation's natural resources for the simple reason that they hoped themselves to exploit them for their own ultimate profit. Because in those days national forests and monuments could be created by executive order and did not need congressional sanction, Congress could not prevent the President from setting them aside, but it could withhold funds for personnel to supervise and maintain the forests and monuments and was ever ready to seek schemes to prevent or discourage the President from exercising this power.

The lobbyists worked in fertile soil, as most members of both houses of Congress opposed restrictions on the use of public lands. In this they reflected the views of the majority of their constituents. In order to hold in check potential backsliders among the legislators the lobbyists skillfully stirred up people in the home districts. So long as public lands continued to be open for grazing, hunting, and the occasional cutting of timber for home consumption, the only concern of nearby homesteaders was to keep outsiders from encroaching on what they regarded as an exclusively neighborhood preserve. But when the government sought to close land to all use, including use by local residents, the small landowners joined with the large corporations in opposing the government's land withdrawal policy.

In fairness to those who fought the withdrawal from use of public lands suitable for grazing, lumbering, or mining, it should be noted that their view had historic sanction. The chance to acquire land had been one of the main motives in the settlement of the American continent from the days of Jamestown and Plymouth onward. Settlers, whether on the eastern seaboard or in the hinterland that stretched from the Appalachians to the Pacific, were land-hungry, and when they homesteaded they planned to do what they wished with their land, without interference from local or national governments. Farmers might quarrel with hunters about the use of nearby public lands. Ranchers might claim that grazing took precedence over hunting, and might insist on exclusive—and free—grazing rights on the public domain for themselves—but not for their rivals, and, in particular, not for the hated sheepherders. Lumbermen looked on the forests greedily, eager to cut trees whether or not they owned title to the land on which the trees grew. Prospectors who tramped brush land, deserts, and mountains in search of minerals took for granted that what they staked out would be theirs.

That government might refuse to patent their claims was unthinkable. All these individual or corporate predators, large or small, were outraged at any suggestion that there is a public interest which transcends that of individual appropriators. They were particularly bitter against those who frankly contended that the federal government had not only the right but the duty to dispose of public land on some basis other than that of "finders is keepers." They likewise questioned or denied the right of the federal government to control the use of rivers and streams in the interest of persons other than those who directly or indirectly sought to monopolize them.

TR's interest in the conservation of natural resources was, of course, traceable to his first-hand knowledge of the West and its problems. None of his predecessors had had his keen awareness of the role of these resources—awareness based not alone on study but on having been through many of the remaining wilderness areas in the country and on experience as a frontier landowner in the last decade of the passing of the old West. As an avid hunter TR knew the need to save the nation's game. As a one-time cowpuncher he knew the value of being able to graze stock on public lands—especially if no fee was charged for the grazing right. But he was aware not only of the injustice in letting a few men have sole use of public lands for grazing but also of the destructive effects of overgrazing. As a landowner who had suffered from alternate droughts and floods he was sure that if streams could be controlled in their courses and their water impounded, farming could be more profitable and water power could be harnessed for productive purposes. With the logic of practical experience he saw—and proclaimed—the close interrelationship of forest protection, including the prevention of overgrazing—water supplies, including the building of dams for irrigation and the development of hydroelectric power—the prevention of erosion and exhaustion of the soil, and the preservation of wild life. When he spoke of conservation he had these multiple uses of the public land in mind.

It was TR's—and the nation's—good fortune that among the officials of the McKinley administration had been three men, Gifford Pinchot, F. H. Newell and W. J. McGee, who not only knew the public domain well, but also had clear ideas as to how public lands might best be used for future generations. While TR was governor at Albany, Pinchot and Newell had helped him formulate New York State's conservation policies. In Washington Pinchot became Chief Forester and Newell was Director of the Geological Survey. McGee was not only an ardent conservationist, but also an anthropologist, a geologist, and a hydrologist. In addition he had the gift of pungent speech. It is to him that is attributed the obvious—but until his day unrecognized—proposition that every river system is a unit from its source to its mouth, and should be treated as such.[1] Pinchot quoted McGee as having defined the objectives of a sound conservation policy as "the use of the natural resources for the greatest good for the greatest number for the longest time."[2] McGee also insisted that monopoly of natural resources was only less dangerous to the public welfare than their actual destruction. All three men placed the interests of the public, present and future, above those persons whose aim was to consume existing resources as fast as possible for their own gain.

Pinchot had been a friend of TR since the early nineties. A dedicated crusader by instinct and training, he became a shrewd political manipulator and a skilled and dramatic publicist in behalf of the cause of saving the nation's resources. His main concern was forestry, and as one of the few Americans up to the end of the nineteenth century who had studied forestry in Europe his stress was on long-range use. This meant not only selective cutting, but reforestation. It also meant the use of efficient lumbering techniques and the elimination of forest wastes so as to lessen the danger of fire. Control implied supervision, which, in turn, implied trained foresters as supervisors and rangers. The key was planning, which presupposed efficiency and farsightedness as well as powers of enforcement. The then prevailing practices of lumbermen were based on reckless, quick, and complete destruction of all available timber. In their place Pinchot fought for long-range yields. Instead of unrestricted exploitation he sought to protect natural resources by selective use rather than by following the simpler but unproductive policy of those whose idea of conservation was to exclude all activities on national forest lands other than sightseeing.

Pinchot spoke for scientific forest management on private as well as public land and preached the doctrine that long-range scientific planning could be profitable for the lumber interests as a whole. He urged the need of fire protection on private as well as on public lands. Basically his concept of conservation was utilitarian. This idea appealed also to TR, who on numerous occasions phrased it as he did in his speech at Osawotamie, Kansas, in 1910, that "conservation means development as much as it does protection."

Even unfriendly historians and biographers admit the effectiveness of TR's support of the conservation movement. This movement was a natural reaction against the abuses that had grown out of the historic fact that since the early days of the Republic, the federal government, which held title to nearly all of the public domain within the present area of the continental United States, had been free and easy in disposing of public lands even after the passage of the Homestead Act of 1862. This act fixed the maximum allotment to any homesteader of 160 acres of surveyed public domain. It was followed by other acts establishing even more generous conditions under which timber and mineral rights on public lands might be acquired. And yet as late as 1900 no good survey of the public domain had been made, nor had lands been classified as to use (i.e., whether for farming, grazing, lumbering, mining, etc.) nor did government employees either in Washington or in the field have personal knowledge of more than very small bits of the public domain.

It is true that a good many million acres had been set aside as national forests, but there was no personnel to police these forests or even to perform the simple function of preventing the erection of fences by individual stockmen whose purpose was to exclude rival stockmen from grazing cattle or sheep on the portions of the public domain which these individuals had appropriated for their own profitable use. The extent of the administrative disorganization in Washington may be judged from the fact that although national forests were under the administration of the Department of the Interior no one in that department had any knowledge of forestry. The only two trained foresters in the employ of the federal government at the turn of the century were in the Department of Agriculture, and these two men had neither jurisdiction over, nor access to, any of the national forest lands. As TR phrased it in his autobiography: "forests and foresters had nothing whatever to do with each other."[3]

There were further complications, in that water rights were legally vested in the states—even water rights on federally owned lands. The federal government could dispose of these lands, but it could not convey the water rights without which most of these lands would be relatively valueless. When finally legislation in behalf of reclamation was introduced into Congress shortly after TR became President, he had to use all the influence at his command in order to prevent the advocates of states' rights inserting into the draft of the bill a clause to the effect that no reclamation project could be undertaken without the consent of the governor of the state within which the project was located. This would have given a state the power to veto a federal project. As the conservation movement gained momentum the advocates of states' rights, often supported by corporate interests that could more effectively dominate state legislatures than Congress, used the states' rights plea to try to block conservation projects of all kinds. Senator Fulton of Oregon procured an amendment to the Agricultural Appropriations bill providing that the President could not set aside any forests in the six northwestern states without the consent of the governors of these states. It is pertinent that in this, one of the most flagrant instances of this sort of partnership in attempted sabotage—TR quietly signed executive orders transferring about 16,000,000 acres of timberlands within these states into national forests only a few days before he signed into law the Agricultural Appropriations bill that sought, among other things, to prevent just this sort of action on his part. It is characteristic of him that when describing this incident in his autobiography he remarked that the opponents of the Forest Service "turned handsprings in their wrath" when they learned how he had legally circumvented them. But according to William Draper Lewis' biography of TR, when a group of the senators who had opposed the enlargement of the forests called on TR to express their resentment at his action in this case their spokesman, Senator Carter of Montana, seeing the mischievous gleam in TR's eyes, "could nurse his wrath no longer. He broke into a hearty laugh, joined by all but one of the other Senators, and extending his hand cordially said: 'It isn't any use! We came to jump all over you, but we can't say anything other than that you put a good one over on us this time!' "

There were also conflicts among opposing civilian interests that kept plaguing the administrators of over-all conservation policies. Small landowners often vied with large corporations for use of public lands. Eastern advocates of game preserves opposed western lumbermen about the ultimate use of uncut forest land. Cattle men did their best to keep sheep off the public range. Cattle and sheep men alike tried to prevent homesteading within the national forests. Often business boosters in frontier towns found themselves at odds with the grazing interests. Stockmen seeking grazing permits on public lands that their rivals also wanted frequently ended up in conflict with the Forest Service, both sides convinced that the federal government, because it controlled public lands, was their main enemy.

TR's concern, based in large measure on the advice of Gifford Pinchot, F. H. Newell and W. J. McGee, was in the first place to establish orderly and efficient administration of the public domain and then to obtain congressional support for broadly based conservation policies. The initial major administrative step was the creation of the Forest Service under the jurisdiction of the Department of Agriculture, and the surveying and classification of public lands. The next step was the establishment of a Reclamation Service, which had as its main objective the control and development of western waterways and the impounding of water for irrigation and for the incidental development of hydroelectric power. Later he also urged the development of navigable inland waterways.

With his fondness for basing policies on general principles, TR insisted in his first annual message that in all matters of conservation of natural resources, public rights must come before private interests.

He looked on the executive as the steward of the public welfare. This concept aroused bitter criticism not only from lawyers but also from members of Congress. It had been originally suggested to TR by George Woodruff, law officer of the Forest Service, a man of whom his friend and classmate Gifford Pinchot wrote that he had "perfect courage, perfect kindness, unending patience, faultless integrity, and at their service a mind of most remarkable power and penetration." TR came to depend much on Woodruff's judgment and advice.

That TR enjoyed exercising stewardship of the public welfare was in keeping with his character and career. He had in him, as has been indicated elsewhere in this volume, the spirit of a crusader combined with a compulsion to get things done. After rereading many of his letters and books I am more than ever impressed with his pragmatism. Whatever he championed politically he sought to implement practically. The need to put an end to the reckless frittering away of the nation's natural resources seemed to him compelling. At the same time the practical side of his character led him to use the current crisis to help to impose long-range policies that would have long-range benefits for the country as a whole. As a shrewd politician he knew that he faced sullen opposition on the part of Congress. Pressures from selfish corporate interests and from shortsighted local leaders would reinforce the parochial and unconstructive attitudes of most of the congressmen and senators from the states in which the most valuable public lands were located, which meant that his only hope of success lay in bringing Congress to heel by building up strong public support for conservation.

One of TR's main concerns about the use of public lands was to encourage homesteaders and settlers. "The policy of the present administration," he wrote to Secretary of Agriculture James Wilson on June 7, 1907, "has steadily been, is now, and will be in the future, to promote and foster actual settling, actual homemaking on the public lands in every possible way." He sought to prevent "the absorption of great areas of the public lands by large owners to the exclusion of honest settlers." He pointed out that among the bitterest opponents of his policy were persons interested in timber and coal lands who wished to monopolize these resources on the public domain, and in particular the big lumber barons—"the managers and owners of those lumber companies which by illegal, fraudulent or unfair methods, have desired to get possession of the valuable timber of the public domain, to skin the land and to abandon it impoverished well-nigh to the point of worthlessness." The purpose of these men, he explained, was to exhaust the resources of the country for their own immediate pecuniary gain. The policy of the government, in contrast, was to put actual settlers on plots of suitable farming land within the reserves, and then "to enforce the law with strict honesty against all men big or little who tried to rob the public domain."

Despite TR's extensive personal knowledge of so many of the problems of conservation he relied heavily on experts such as Pinchot, Newell, and McGee. Furthermore, he resorted freely to the policy of appointing advisory commissions whose functions were to make reports and recommendations to him about the implementation and development of long-range conservation policies. As he got deeper into the over-all problems he sought to enlist the interest of the states by calling a governor's conference, which met in the White House in May, 1908. As an outgrowth of this meeting the President appointed a National Conservation Commission to undertake an inventory of all natural resources. It was divided into four sections—waters, forests, lands, and minerals—each of which had as chairman a senator or congressman. Each section had as secretary one of the ablest among the professional bureaucrats. There was also an executive committee composed of the four section leaders, the four secretaries, and Chief Forester Pinchot as chairman.[4] Congress, however, refused to appropriate funds for the commission and showed increasing resentment against TR's partiality for experts—so much so, in fact, that one of the last acts of Congress just a few weeks before TR left the White House in 1909 was to approve the so-called Tawney Amendment to the Sundry Civil Bill, prohibiting any federal administrative official from aiding the work of any federal commission not authorized by Congress. The obvious intent of Congress was to put an end to the use of commissions in helping to develop national policies. The gesture was partly spiteful and partly an expression by members of Congress of their understandable resentment of the kind of executive independence that TR had consistently shown as President. It also reflected the traditional dislike of politicians for experts in any field. They sensed that the use of experts in the formulation of governmental policies might lead to a new concept in American politics and government—that nationwide planning in many fields was essential and that such planning was beyond the scope and experience of men who by law and custom represented regional and even parochial interests and who had neither the knowledge, the concern, nor the legal responsibility to take a nationwide view of political, economic, and social problems.

Valuable as was TR's emphasis on administrative, political, and utilitarian aspects of conservation, this practical approach should not be interpreted to mean that he failed to sense to the full the esthetic and spiritual importance of saving the nation's natural beauties. Quite the contrary. His love of natural beauty in all its forms—scenery, sun and sky, flowers, trees, birds and other wild life—was ever present in his concern about conservation. This sensitivity was, in fact, one of the interesting facets of his many-sided personality. He was not particularly responsive to the arts. Musically he was tone deaf. Even his interest in poetry was inclined to be in rhythm and in the exploits of heroes rather than in the literary skill of the authors. And yet, although city-born and city-bred, he was deeply responsive to the compelling wonders of the wilderness.

While the appeal to him of the ruggedness of portions of rural America unquestionably lay partly in its challenge—in the practical, therapeutical rewards that the wilderness had given him in helping him to complete the transformation of his initially delicate physical frame into a robust and immensely powerful body and in the attendant satisfactions that he derived from the many proofs of his resourcefulness, courage, and endurance—yet he seemed to find in the wilderness a source of replenishment of his spiritual strength. No one who had been with him on hunting or camping trips could fail to note his frequently expressed deep delight at some unusual bit of landscape or color. I was interested to read that even Henry F. Pringle, whose biography of TR is tinged with skepticism, sensed the significance of Dakota in his life. Referring to TR's trip through the Little

Missouri country during the campaign for the vice-presidency, Pringle described him sitting alone on the platform of the observation car after his train had left Medora and noted that when a member of the party entered the candidate's car looking for him, the door to the observation platform was blocked by a colored Pullman porter. "The governor don't want to see nobody for a while," the porter explained apologetically.[5] TR obviously was engaged in what was for him a rare experience—indulging in reveries of the past. That he wanted to be alone while going through this stretch of country that had meant so much to him in his young manhood suggests the depth of his sense of the spiritual values of the wilderness. I am certain that one of the main reasons that his work in conservation seemed to him so important was the realization of the need for making it possible for countless millions of Americans to derive from their own contacts with unspoiled segments of the American scene the same kind of solace and satisfaction that had been his when he ranched in the Bad Lands, hunted mountain sheep in the Grand Tetons, rode with John Burroughs through Yellowstone, camped in Yosemite with John Muir, or, as during our summer in Arizona, when he savored to the full the magnificence of the North Rim of the Grand Canyon and the almost unbelievable perfection of Rainbow Natural Bridge. These restricted areas are, of course, only remnants of the continent's once supposedly unlimited natural riches. But it was because of his foresight and shrewdness in paving the way for the preservation of such resources that the conservation movement was successfully launched in the first decade of the twentieth century.

13

TOWARD WORLD POWER

DURING THE LAST TWO DECADES of the nineteenth century, when TR unknowingly was completing his preparation for the presidency, world peace seemed secure—peace based on Britain's supremacy of sea power. As Captain (later Admiral) Alfred Thayer Mahan indicated in his book, *The Influence of Sea Power on History*, the concept of sea power rests on the close interrelationship between industry, trade, a merchant fleet, and naval power. A great industrial nation depends on commerce with other nations. Overseas trade, in turn, depends on a merchant marine able to carry the nation's imports and exports in war as in peace. Such a merchant marine depends for its protection on a strong navy. This means not only powerful ships of war and well trained personnel, but also strategically located bases at home and abroad, where ships can be docked for repairs and where supplies of fuel, water, ammunition, food, and other necessaries may be stockpiled. The exercise of sea power on a global scale implies not only the control of natural bottlenecks of sea travel, such as the narrows of the English Channel, the Straits of Gibraltar, and the passage from the Indian Ocean into the Pacific by way of Singapore, but also the unhampered use of the Suez and Panama canals. The importance of a merchant marine in time of war may be judged from the fact that Germany used submarines so effectively to harass allied merchant shipping in World War I that Germany came very near winning that war—and winning it primarily by the near destruction of Britain's life lines.

Mahan's book on sea power, as I have indicated in Chapter VI, greatly impressed the Kaiser. Since his accession to the throne in 1888 this somewhat jittery monarch had been chafing under the ambitions of his war lords and admirals to see Germany outbuild Britain's navy and to have the German mercantile marine take over from the British merchant fleet as much of the carrying of the world's commerce as possible. Germany was definitely "on the make." Great Britain, equally definitely, wished simply to continue holding its long established world supremacy, based on sea power. The lesson was plain—that just as England had risen to world dominance through sea power so Germany could take England's place if it could not only challenge, but actually overthrow, England's sea power. German industrialists backed the new German imperialism based on a powerful navy and large merchant marine. More naval and cargo vessels meant more work for German shipyards, more consumption of coal, steel, and machinery and greater profits for mine owners, industrialists, shipbuilders, and financiers. Publicists swelled the chorus of Germany's right to a "place in the sun." The Kaiser, photogenic in his succession of different helmets and uniforms, became a popular figurehead. Susceptible to flattery, with illusions as to his own intellectual gifts, he proved a useful tool for the small group of ambitious and determined naval, military and industrial leaders who were dedicated to the ideal of making Germany the dominant imperial power in the world. Only Britain's navy stood in the way of Germany's ambitions.

The British, accustomed since the battle of Waterloo to expand their overseas trade and influence unchallenged—especially outside of Europe and the two Americas—acted on the prideful assumption that what was good for the British Empire was good for the world. They hailed British imperialism as bringing to "backward" peoples the "blessings" of modern civilization. The fact that British merchants, industrialists, and financiers were the chief beneficiaries of nineteenth-century expansionism and colonialism was offset by the comforting thought that part of the tradition of the British colonial service was that British officials of all ranks had a sense of obligation toward the alien peoples who came under their dominion. The success of British imperialism, which, it should be noted in passing, was paralleled by the efficient and humane rule of the Dutch in the Netherlands East Indies, encouraged France, Germany, Belgium, and Italy to seek colonies in Africa and (Italy excepted) "spheres of influence" in China. Germany in both these continents was a latecomer.

In this world atmosphere of expansionism it is not surprising to find that, as early as May, 1897, TR (only a few weeks after becoming Assistant Secretary of the Navy) wrote Captain Mahan confidentially, saying that if he had his way, the United States would annex the Hawaiian Islands "tomorrow." He went on to explain that "if that is impossible, I would establish a protectorate over them. I believe that we should build the Nicaraguan Canal at once, and in the meantime that we should build a dozen new battleships, half of them on the Pacific Coast." Later in the same letter he referred to "big problems" in the West Indies also. "Until we definitely turn Spain out of these Islands (and if I had my way that would be done tomorrow) we will always be menaced by trouble there. We should acquire the Danish Islands, and by turning Spain out should serve notice that no strong European power, and especially not Germany, should be allowed to gain a foothold by supplanting some weak European power. I do not fear England; Canada is a hostage for her good behavior; but I do fear some other powers."[1]

These ideas, of course, were not original with TR, nor were they held exclusively by himself and Mahan. But they should be considered against the background of America's traditional isolation and noninvolvement in world politics that traced back to Washington's Farewell Address. The population of the United States at the end of the nineteenth century was little more than 75,000,000. These people were more interested in the development of the natural resources of the American continent than in the relations of the United States Government with other nations. They knew little about world politics and were as indifferent to, as they were ignorant of, the basic instability that prevailed from Mexico and the Caribbean southward to Tierra del Fuego. So long as no European or Asiatic power intervened in the internal affairs of any of the nations of the western hemisphere—as France had done in Mexico in the 1860s and as Germany and Britain had threatened to do at the turn of the century—the American people took a pharisaical view of international affairs, thanking God that the United States was not as other nations. This pious reaction spared them the tedium of trying to understand Europe's power politics—which is probably just as well, because in world affairs the American government at that time carried little weight and had only a small and antiquated navy and virtually no army.

In weighing with the benefit of hindsight the views that TR expressed to Mahan, it is pertinent to note that within a relatively short time after TR wrote this letter the United States annexed Hawaii; Spain was turned out of Cuba and Puerto Rico; the United States acquired the Danish islands; at least one move that might have led the German occupation of South American territory was effectively discouraged; and the construction of a trans-Isthmian canal was undertaken by the United States Government—not in Nicaragua but in Panama. In all but the acquisition of the Danish West Indies, TR played an instrumental part, for which he was roundly denounced by the leading "liberals" of his day and by many of their successors. It would be interesting to know how many of his critics would un-annex

Hawaii, fill up the Canal, return the Virgin Islands to Denmark, and give Cuba and Puerto Rico back to Spain. It may be assumed that even those who welcome Communist intervention in Latin America would have been opposed to the occupation of parts of Venezuela by Imperial Germany.

All of which is another way of suggesting that the objectives for which TR, Mahan, and others were striving at the turn of the century have long been accepted as sound. Doubtless TR, who handled most of the diplomatic negotiations in person, exposed himself to criticism as to methods and procedures. There are always plenty of Monday morning quarterbacks ready to explain in detail just how a particular game should have been played. But TR knew what he wanted and how to get it. The records of his intercession in three major diplomatic crises—the threat of Germany in 1902 to occupy parts of Venezuela to satisfy financial claims, the bringing together of Japan and Russia in 1905 to end the war between those nations, and the Algeciras Conference about Morocco in 1906—show that he was astute and effective as a negotiator. His task was made easier by the fact that he had long been on terms of personal friendship with a number of key European diplomats, notably the French ambassador in Washington, Jules Jusserand; the German ambassador, Speck von Sternburg; and the future British ambassador to Washington, Spring-Rice, who was in close touch with influential men in the British foreign office. TR also had known well for years leading American diplomats such as John Hay and Elihu Root, both of whom served him as Secretary of State; Joseph H. Choate and Whitelaw Reid, who successively held the post of American Ambassador in London; and Henry White, who knew well many of the diplomats and political leaders on the continent. Shrewd, courteous and friendly, TR owed a part at least of his success to what the late Lewis Einstein, for years a distinguished member of the American foreign service, described as a combination of "the skill of a politician and the learning of an historian with the principle of a cowboy never to draw his gun unless prepared to shoot."[2]

The value of these personal contacts should not be underestimated. In the late nineteenth century and the first decade of the twentieth century, government in most of Europe—especially the conduct of foreign affairs—was still largely in the hands of members of a small number of families in each country who owed much of their influence to inherited rank and family connections. Regardless of nationality the members of this group had been brought up in a tradition of public service. Nearly all had the advantages of exceptionally good education and of having inherited wealth. Many had spent their childhood in foreign countries where their parents had been stationed. While TR had no ties of kinship with any of these diplomatic leaders in Europe, he knew about many of them and had had friendly relations with some in his Washington days before the presidency, and on his travels to Europe. They liked him and looked on him as a gentleman and a scholar, which was more important before World War I than it is now.

As I was only sixteen when TR left the White House I had no personal knowledge of his conduct of foreign affairs. But from my college years onward I often heard him speak of incidents with which he had dealt. One, in particular, still stands out clearly in my memory. This is the Venezuela incident of December, 1902, when the German government was preparing to occupy parts of Venezuela so as to force the government of that country to pay its German creditors on defaulted loans. The story as I heard him tell it on a number of occasions was that when rumors of impending naval action in Venezuela by Germany increased, TR sent for the German ambassador, Von Holleben, and asked him to inform his government that he hoped that Germany would consent to submit the disagreement to arbitration. The ambassador replied that this was impossible. When TR elaborated his reasons for requesting arbitration and

Von Holleben continued to insist that it was out of the question, TR told the ambassador that if no notification for arbitration came within a specified number of days—as I recall it, TR in telling us about the incident said ten days—the American fleet would be sent to the Venezuelan coast to prevent Germany from taking possession of any Venezuelan territory. The ambassador replied that this would have "serious consequences"—which, in diplomatic parlance meant that it might lead to war. Whereupon TR called the ambassador's attention to the fact that in the event of a conflict with the United States there were few places where Germany would be at a greater disadvantage than in the Caribbean. When, a few days later, Von Holleben called on the President on another matter and made no mention of the proposed arbitration of the Venezuelan dispute, TR asked him if his government had yet sent any reply to his request. Von Holleben answered in the negative. TR then said that under the circumstances he would order Admiral Dewey to sail for Venezuela with the American fleet twenty-four hours ahead of the time he had originally specified. The ambassador seemed much upset and insisted, as he had on his previous visit, that arbitration was out of the question. But a few hours ahead of the expiration of the new time limit set by the President the ambassador called at the White House to say that the Emperor would be much pleased if TR himself would undertake the arbitration. TR said that he did not think that this would be appropriate and suggested instead that the Hague Tribunal serve as arbiter, to which the Kaiser consented. Both privately and publicly TR expressed his appreciation of what the Kaiser had done and praised him for his statesmanship.

Some of TR's critics have questioned the veracity of TR's account of this incident. As I find it hard to believe that he would deliberately misrepresent and distort his part in this affair when telling his children and their cousins and friends about it, I reread a number of accounts of the incident. These included

TR's own version in his letter to William Roscoe Thayer, dated April 21, 1916; Henry F. Pringle's grudging admission in his biography of TR that the former President might have been right, but that TR's memory obviously was at fault and that very probably his intention was to deceive; and Howard K. Beale's carefully documented analysis which clearly indicates that, barring a few minor details, TR's account as written to Thayer (which parallels the account that I heard him give) is trustworthy.

To some of the critics it apparently seemed that TR had issued an "ultimatum" and that the Kaiser had backed down. Presumably they regarded the former as discreditable and the latter as unbelievable. To others, TR, when he wrote the letter in 1916, appeared to be suffering from excessive anti-Germanism that the critics attributed to his quarrel with Wilson about America's attitude toward participation in World War I. This interpretation overlooks the fact that in his published corre-spendence there are many examples of TR's distrust of German intentions in the Caribbean and elsewhere in Latin America running back to the 1890s and early 1900s.

To me there is a simple and logical explanation: that when TR realized that the German ambassador had not taken him at his word about sending the American fleet to Venezuela on a specified date, he advanced the date of Admiral Dewey's sailing in the belief that this would convince the German government of the firmness of his intentions. This is in keeping with his character and is the practical maneuvering of a man who neither bluffed nor could be bluffed. If for years he said nothing public about his tactics the most likely reason is that, having attained his objective of inducing the German government to arbitrate, he was glad to give the impression publicly that the initiative for the amicable settlement came from the Kaiser.

My only diary entries about TR and Panama refer to his having expressed the opinion that his part in getting the Panama

Canal built under American auspices was the most important single contribution that he had made as President. This statement appears in various writings and speeches of his. It gains interest because while individual critics have differed among each other as to various other acts of his of which they disapprove, they are nearly unanimous in their criticism of his role in this instance. Furthermore, several friendly biographers have been critical of his procedure in this case even when they have approved his objective.

Although the Panama incident has been the subject of many articles and a number of books, his compulsive objective deserves restating. He was convinced that an interocean canal, either across the Panama Isthmus or through Nicaragua, was a primary and fundamental need in the development of the naval power of the United States. It would also be of great commercial benefit to the United States by bringing the two coasts within easy reach of each other by sea, and by facilitating the development of West Coast shipping with Europe, and the commerce of the East Coast with the nations of the west coast of Latin America.

TR insisted that not only should the United States build the canal, but that it should control it and fortify it and, in the event of war, should have the right to exclude enemy vessels. As he put it in a letter to Mahan written even before he had become Vice-President: "I do not see why we should dig the canal if we are not to fortify it so as to insure its being used for ourselves and against our foes in time of war."[3] To this relatively simple objective he clung from beginning to end—and before it was attained a fifty-year-old treaty with Great Britain would have to be modified or abrogated; the right to build the canal, which had been vested in a French company by Colombia, would have to be transferred to the United States; and the American government would have to embark on a gigantic engineering and construction job such as it had never before attempted.

The reason why the treaty with Great Britain had to be modified or abrogated was that this document, referred to by historians as the Clayton-Bulwer treaty, which had been signed in 1850, declared that neither the American nor the British government would ever obtain exclusive control over a trans-isthmian canal, nor would either government fortify such a canal or any territory in its vicinity. Throughout 1899 John Hay, then Secretary of State, negotiated with the British ambassador in Washington, Sir Julian Pauncefote, a treaty known as the *first* Hay-Pauncefote treaty, which provided that Great Britain renounced joint rights to the canal that the United States might build, but the provision of the Clayton-Bulwer treaty to the effect that the United States could not fortify the canal was retained. As Samuel Flagg Bemis put it in his *Diplomatic History of the United States* the United States, under the terms of this new treaty could "go to the expense of constructing this canal and maintaining it, but could have no special advantage of any kind, even in case it were engaged in war; in time of war an enemy might sail its fleet right through the canal to attack San Francisco or Savannah."[4]

TR, who was at the time governor of New York, disapproved of this treaty. As he put it in a letter to John Hay a few days after the signing of the treaty: "If that canal is open to warships of an enemy it is a menace to us in time of war; it is an added burden, an additional strategic point to be guarded by our fleet. If fortified by us it becomes one of the most potent sources of our possible sea strength. Unless so fortified it strengthens against us every nation whose fleet is larger than ours. . . . our fleet would have to watch it, and therefore do the work which a fort could do; and which it could do much better."[5] In a public statement made only a few days before he wrote this letter to Hay, TR said: "I most earnestly hope that the pending treaty as to the future treatment of the Isthmian canal will not be ratified unless amended so as to provide that the canal when built shall be wholly under the control of the United States, alike in peace and war. This seems to be vital from the standpoint of the Monroe doctrine."[6]

The first Hay-Pauncefote treaty was amended in the United States Senate and the amendments proved unacceptable to the British. This treaty was therefore superseded by what is called the *second* Hay-Pauncefote treaty, ratified on February 21, 1902, which, among other things, omitted the prohibition against the fortification of the canal and which had TR's endorsement.

The next diplomatic step was the negotiation of a treaty with Colombia, which at that time owned the Isthmus of Panama, having as its purpose to provide for the transfer to the United States of the legal title for the construction of the canal, which Colombia had granted to the French Panama Canal Company. This treaty also provided that Colombia would lease to the United States a strip of land across the Isthmus through which the canal would be built. The United States agreed to pay Colombia $10,000,000, together with an annuity of $250,000 a year beginning nine years after the ratification of the treaty. But the Colombian senate failed to ratify it, because, according to Bemis, the senators "thought they might get more money both from the United States and from the Panama Company."[7]

Nonratification by Colombia presented the government in Washington with at least five choices: 1) To offer to pay more to Colombia; 2) to delay further consideration of building a canal at Panama until such time as a new agreement was negotiated with Colombia; 3) to abandon the Panama route and instead to complete negotiations with Nicaragua and Costa Rica for a Nicaraguan Canal; 4) to await the possibility of a separatist movement in Panama province—a movement already supported by a substantial element there; or, 5) to occupy the Canal Zone by force.

TR's natural impatience, together with his deep conviction that the canal must be built as soon as possible, inclined him against the second possibility. While he had originally favored a Nicaraguan canal the latest reports of his engineers had convinced him that the Panama route was preferable. An instinctive dislike of being blackmailed prevented his considering offering to pay Colombia a larger sum. The choice was thus narrowed to seizing the proposed canal zone by force or waiting to see if the rumors of a growing movement in Panama to make that Colombian province into an independent republic were well founded. That TR had been approached by persons wishing him to encourage the independence of Panama is apparent from numerous statements of his to the effect that it would be improper for him to support any such movement.

It was at this stage of the incident that Philippe Bunau-Varilla, former French engineer of the Panama Canal Company, apparently took over the direction of events. He has been depicted as a soldier of fortune, an adventurer, and a schemer—which, I think, is unjust to a hard-headed, practical French businessman who happened to have a passionate interest in seeing the Panama Canal on which he had worked as an engineer, carried through to completion. While I had not known him in 1903 I met him a dozen years later when I was a young attaché at the American Embassy in Paris, and thenceforth saw him whenever I passed through that city. He and I were on the same French liner when I returned from France in 1924 and spent many hours together as he poured out his views on the war, the need to transform the lock canal at Panama into a sea-level canal, and many other interesting matters. He had all the charming qualities of the cultivated upper-class Frenchmen, with a scholarly background and broad interests. He was in his mid-sixties at the time, and even though he had a wooden leg, his energy seemed as irrepressible as his enthusiasm. TR described him as "a keen, grey-eyed French duellist, who would look you straight in the eye."[8] To this I would add that he had a square brow and jaw, a closely cropped moustache, and a delicately chiseled nose.

As a young man Bunau-Varilla had become a protégé of John Bigelow, who had been one of the owners of the *New York Evening Post* before President Lincoln appointed him as minister to France. Through Bigelow he had come to know such men as Mark Hanna and John Hay, and through these two had met TR. With his many connections in Panama, and as representative, at this particular time, of the French Panama Canal Company, he was in an excellent position to encourage and guide those Panamanians who believed that they would be the gainers if Panama became an independent republic and facilitated the construction of the canal by the American government. As a man of wide experience he was fully aware of the delicacy of his position, and I am sure that he must have been scrupulously careful in his talks with Hay and TR not to say anything about his plans that might cause them any embarrassment. While I base this largely on my own contacts with the man, there is confirmation in Max Farrand's report that TR, describing Bunau-Varilla's visit to the White House, said: "There might just as well have been a dictaphone in the room," i.e., everyone talked with the greatest discretion. The Frenchman predicted a revolution in Panama and said he would like to know if the United States would prevent Colombian troops from landing, and, watching the President keenly, said: "I don't suppose you can say." To this TR replied: "I cannot." Bunau-Varilla then asked him if he would protect Colombian interests. To which TR replied in substance: "I cannot say that. All I can say is that Colombia by her action [in failing to ratify the treaty] has forfeited any claim upon the United States and I have no use for a government that would do what that government had done." Whereupon, according to this report by TR ten years later, Bunau-Varilla rose and said, "Good afternoon, Mr. President," and left. Nothing definite was said, but I am sure that each knew what the other had in mind.[9]

Bunau-Varilla's task in guiding the Panamanian revolution was complicated not so much by problems of inducing the province to secede as by the multiplication of revolutionary groups anxious to lead the movement. So many Panamanians saw potential advantages to themselves in separation from Colombia that even if TR had been tempted to intervene it would almost surely have been superfluous. To repeat TR's expressive phrase that he used to Coolidge and Farrand (and also in a few other references to the Panama incident) it was not a case of his giving the signal to start a revolution in Panama, but of raising his foot —that is, to cease stamping out fuses.

While there is no evidence that the American government sparked the revolution there is nothing to show that it sought to discourage the would-be revolutionists—nor is there any reason why it should have done so. But what is beyond dispute is that the American government prevented Colombian troops from landing in Panama to put down the revolution, which, as Bemis noted, "guaranteed the success of the insurrection; in effect it completed it."[10] Three days later the government of the United States recognized the *de facto* government of the new Republic of Panama. Within a few months the leading European nations and all the Latin American countries except Colombia recognized the independence of the new republic.

Doubtless it could have been done differently. Perhaps it should have been. But impatience was one of TR's strong traits, and it may be generalized that the greater the importance he attached to an objective the greater seems to have been his impatience when embarked on achieving it. The evidence is conclusive that he regarded the building of an interocean canal as of urgent importance and that he was determined that nothing would stop him from getting it built. He was probably correct when he said in 1918 that if, instead of acting as he did, he had submitted the matter to the Senate, "we would have had a half century of discussion, and perhaps the Panama Canal. I preferred we should have the Panama Canal first and the half century of discussion afterward. And now instead of discussing the canal before it was built, which would have been harmful, they merely discuss me—a discussion which I regard with benign interest."[11]

His supporters believed that he had been shrewd. Criticism centered on procedure—which prompted from the whimsical John Hay the remark that this reminded him of the instruction of a western outlaw chief: "Kill him, but kill him easy!"[12] Doubtless the discussion about what TR did will continue. But the canal was opened to traffic in 1914—a little later, perhaps, than he had hoped—but five years before his death.

In another diplomatic incident TR's meticulous concern for procedure was beyond criticism, even though his objective marked such a drastic departure from the traditional American policy of noninvolvement in the affairs of Europe that, had it become public at that time, it would undoubtedly have brought bitter criticism on him. It is significant that in his *autobiography* he does not mention the incident.

I refer to his participation in calling the Algeciras Conference about Moroccan affairs in January, 1906, and his subsequent representation at this conference by Henry White, assisted by J. R. Gummere and Lewis Einstein. The conference grew out of one of Europe's war scares of the kind that led ultimately to the First World War. This one had its origin in maneuverings by the German Kaiser to strengthen the position of Germany with respect to France following the serious decline of Russia's influence in Europe resulting from its disastrous war with Japan. Russia, it will be recalled, was already in partnership with France, and France had made an agreement with Great Britain settling numerous points of dispute between the two countries. As TR put it in a letter to Ambassador Jusserand on April 25, 1906: "In last May and June the relations between . . . [Germany and France] were so strained that war was imminent." He then went on to state his opinion that "probably the only way it could have been avoided was by an international conference, and such a conference could only have been held on terms compatible with France's honour and dignity."

The story of the entire incident is given in a forty-page letter that TR addressed to Whitelaw Reid, then American ambassador in London, under date of April 28, 1906. It was marked "Absolutely private and confidential," but has been included in the eight-volume edition of TR's letters published in the early 1950s. This letter contains memoranda and texts of communications, most of which passed between TR and his two close friends, Baron Speck von Sternburg, the German ambassador, and M. Jusserand, the French ambassador, in Washington.

TR's primary role centered on inducing the governments of the nations concerned about the future of Morocco to meet in conference to discuss a settlement by diplomacy in order to avoid resort to war. Particular interest attaches to TR's very full account of the entire incident in that it shows not only his resourcefulness, in inducing the Kaiser on the one hand and the French government on the other to agree to a reasonable discussion, but also his shrewdness, in giving credit to the Kaiser and to the head of the French government for achievements that had been due primarily to TR's own initiative. He had a succession of visits from Speck and from Jusserand throughout the entire negotiations, and served, in fact, as direct intermediary between the Kaiser and the French government. Of Speck, TR wrote that "loyal though Speck was to his government, both Root and I became convinced that down in his heart the honest, brave little gentleman did not really believe Germany was acting as she should act." Of Jusserand he said in the same letter to Whitelaw Reid: "I was entirely sure of France only when I could act direct through Jusserand, who rang true under any and all circumstances." In his letter to Jusserand to which I have already referred above, he amplified the help that Jusserand had given him and said that he could have done little or nothing "if I had not possessed entire confidence alike in your unfailing soundness of judgment and in your high integrity of personal conduct. . . . If, in these delicate Morocco negotiations, I had not been able to treat you with the absolute frankness and confidence that I did, no good results could possibly have been obtained, and this frankness and confidence were rendered possible only because of the certainty that you would do and advise what was wisest to be done and advised, and that you would treat all that was said and done between us two as a gentleman of the highest honour treats what is said and done in the intimate personal relations of life."[13] It is interesting to note in contrast that the close and sympathetic exchanges that he was able to have with the German and French ambassadors were absent in his dealing with the British ambassador, Sir Mortimer Durand. To Whitelaw Reid TR remarked that Durand "seems to have a brain of about eight guinea pig-power," and went on to describe him as a "worthy creature of mutton-suet consistency."

Einstein, who, as I said, was present at the Algeciras Conference as secretary, noted that "Alone, unaided and unsuspected, Roosevelt in the Moroccan crisis gave the measure of his diplomatic skill. Congress knew nothing, the country knew nothing, his own agents knew nothing, the world knew nothing, of all he had done to preserve peace. . . . His steps were not particularly subtle or deep. They were the obvious intelligent steps which a capable man of experience, tact and good intention, occupying a commanding position, courageous and confident in himself, unafraid of responsibility, and above all a gentleman at heart, would have taken, for only a gentleman would afterward have kept silence."[14]

Of course TR took a risk. Had his part been made public he would have been bitterly criticized by liberals as well as conservatives. But he felt that he was justified to intervene in behalf of preserving the peace of the world. Had war broken out then instead of eight years later his position might have been embarrassing. But so thorough was his knowledge of world politics that he realized that the United States, even though relatively not well armed, was in a sense able to tip the balance of power as it wished.

As I look back on TR as I knew him and on the many books about him which I have read, I think that his part in the Algeciras Conference was, in fact, one of the decisive episodes in his life. It gave him intimate knowledge of the personalities determining the events that were destined to plunge the world into a catastrophic war—knowledge such as he could not possibly have had otherwise, and such as no other American, regardless of his position and influence, then possessed. When the guns of August, 1914, began firing he was—or so the world thought—at the lowest point in his career. Physically he was the victim of tropical diseases incurred in the Brazilian jungles. Politically he was the defeated candidate of a lost cause. Socially he was excoriated by former friends and admirers who deplored his part in the 1912 campaign. In fact, he had become a leader with few followers, a writer with few readers, but—which must have been hardest to bear—with eyes still telescopically clear. TR had a vast knowledge of world affairs and a keen awareness of the role that the United States would have to play, and yet in the first years of World War I he faced the frustration of trying to reach the ears of a people who gladly closed them to the truths they could not bear to hear and instead were happily lulled into sweet dreams of peace through arbitration treaties devised in ignorance, advocated with cynicism, and destined to be scraps of paper.

TR could be downed, but so long as he lived he could not be counted out. As former President he held back for weeks at the start of World War I from saying anything that might embarrass his successor in the White House. But as he saw the Wilson administration compound blindness with blunders and heard inaction heralded as wisdom and neutrality in thought exalted above right or wrong the crusader in him once more revived. Correctly he foresaw that America could not escape the world conflict. The pragmatist in him translated this fact into a strident call for armament and military preparedness. Over and over again he raised his warning voice, but only slowly—very slowly—did the people respond.

14

CLARITY VS. CONFUSION

THE FIRST WORLD WAR dramatized the contrasts between Theodore Roosevelt and Woodrow Wilson—contrasts in knowledge, in objectives, in methods, and in concepts of the presidency. TR had known and for seven years had dealt with the leading statesmen of Europe and with some of Europe's most influential military and naval men. He had an expert's knowledge of European history and of the struggle for power to which German writers gave the name of "*Realpolitik.*" He had helped delay war in Europe in 1906. He had been a weekend guest of the mercurial German Kaiser, and had reviewed the Imperial army with him. He had discussed naval problems with Grand Admiral von Tirpitz. He had spent two days alone with Britain's knowledgeable Foreign Secretary, Sir Edward Grey, in the New Forest, discussing birds, politics, and poetry, and had had long talks about Britain's military unpreparedness with the forthright old British Field Marshal, Lord Roberts, who, more than any other Englishman of the prewar decade had tried to waken the British government and public to Germany's ambitions and intentions. I remember TR showing me a quotation from a speech Lord Roberts made in 1912 about the attitude of Germany's leaders (I quote it from Frederick Scott Oliver's *Ordeal by Battle*): "In their heart of hearts they know, every man of them, that—just as in 1866 [when Prussia attacked Austria] and just as in 1870 [when Germany engineered the Franco-Prussian war]—war will take place the instant the German forces by land and sea are, by their superiority at every point, as certain of victory as anything in human calculations can be made certain. *Germany strikes when Germany's hour has struck.* That is the time-honored policy of her foreign office."[1]

The basic factor in the rivalry of the European nations that led to the First World War was the technological and industrial expansion of Germany relentlessly molded into a policy of world domination by German imperialists, militarists, and publicists. In its simplest form what Germany wanted was not just a "place in the sun," but a *commanding* place in the sun, and Germany was ready—and even eager—to go to war to attain this end, which predicated building a powerful navy and a large merchant marine. No kind of sophistry can alter two basic facts: 1) that Germany in so doing was acting as other nations had acted throughout the previous two centuries in Europe; and, 2) that as success for Germany's plans was only conceivable if Britain's long-established world supremacy as a naval and commercial power could be overthrown, the ultimate objective of the Germans must be to hamstring or destroy the British fleet, which meant, to begin with, the crippling of Britain's allies.

German strategists in 1914 knew as well as did the British high command that the prerequisite to the defeat of Britain was control by the Germans of what historians in the nineteenth century and earlier called the "Low Countries," which meant primarily Belgium and a strip of the coast of France including Calais and Boulogne. Only from here was there a chance of invading England, and without a successful occupation of England that country would be hard to dominate. This was, of course, before the days of air power, and it was based on the premise that France would have to be militarily prevented from coming to England's aid when the cross-channel invasion started. In other words, the sequence of events was: 1) occupation of Belgium; 2) immobilization of France; 3) invasion of England. It is pertinent that in World War II, when German air power was great, the German high command still planned to invade England and made the attempt from the same portion of the Low Countries. So also, three and a quarter centuries earlier, the Spanish Armada had had as its main objective to furnish transportation and protection for an invasion of England based on the Flemish mainland.

Students of military affairs in 1914 were well aware of the basic strategic advantages inherent in the central position of Germany and Austria-Hungary vis-à-vis the peripheral, disjointed alliance of Great Britain, France, and Russia. As early as 1910 TR's friend, Admiral Mahan, had written for the *London Daily Mail* two articles in which he brought out this point and also discussed the advantage to the Central Powers that would accrue from being able to take the initiative as aggressors. There is nothing new or startling in what Mahan stressed. The basic facts were well known to students of world affairs years before 1914. Also well known was the fact that an essential part of Germany's strategy when it declared war would be to move large quantities of troops through Belgium for the double purpose of striking at France's defenses where they were weakest and of gaining control of the stretch of coast of the English Channel from which alone a successful invasion of England could be launched. But it is safe to assume that 99 per cent of the American people were unaware of the strategic significance of Belgium.

On August 3, 1914, as the war was just starting, Admiral Mahan gave a statement to the American press, which because of its perceptiveness and knowledge deserves a brief summation. Starting from the premise that it was unbelievable that Austria would have ventured on the ultimatum to Serbia without previous assurance of German support, he said: "The inference is irresistible that *the substance of the ultimatum* was the *pretext* for a war *already determined* on as soon as a *plausible occasion* offered." [The italics are mine]. He went on to explain that the cause of this predetermination was to be found in the growing strength of Russia as it recovered from its war with Japan, and in the current deficiencies in French armaments. In other words it was an auspicious time for the Central Powers to strike. Indicating that Germany's policy was based on the sure effectiveness of quick, concentrated initial momentum, Mahan suggested that if there were to be a long delay the Germans might go ahead building a sea force equal or superior to that of Great Britain, and that in that case the world would be "confronted by the naval power of a state, not, like Great Britain, sated with territory, but one eager and ambitious for expansion, eager also for influence." In these few words he pointed out one of the most important reasons why the outcome of World War I was of such great concern to the American people and government—that Germany was "on the make," whereas Great Britain sought merely to retain what she already had and that if Germany won we would be faced with an aggressive naval power in place of a satisfied sea power with which we had managed to get along for decades despite many minor quarrels. Especially since the Civil War the British, while they still disliked Americans and regarded them as commercial rivals, had pursued a policy of live-and-let-live. In contrast, Germany in 1914 was eager for expansion and influence, and, as we were soon to learn, ruthless in the pursuit of its aims.

Three days later Mahan was silenced by executive order, as were all officers of the Army and Navy. Whether or not the muzzling impetus came from the President and the Secretary of State or from old-line high-ranking admirals and generals who for years had resented the attention that Mahan had earned by his writings, the White House obviously was aware of and approved the silencing of the expression of opinions of the European war by military and naval experts, no matter how sound and enlightening their statements might be. In this connection it is interesting that at the time of the Moroccan crisis and the Hague Conference in 1906 TR as President wrote Mahan: "I desire to have you have a free hand to discuss in any way you wish the so-called peace proposals. You have a deserved reputation as a publicist which makes this proper from the public standpoint. Indeed, I think it important for you to write just what you think of the matter."[2] When influential persons tried to get the Wilson administration to lift the ban on Mahan's writings in 1914 they met with no success. The nation—and particularly officials of all ranks—must, as Mr. Wilson expressed it, be neutral in thought as well as in deed. As elaborated by his followers this kind of neutrality became virtually neutrality between knowledge and ignorance, between truth and falsehood, as well as between right and wrong—a sort of national cult of Pontius Pilate.

Wilson, in contrast to Roosevelt, was not well-versed in Europe's history and resented as well as disdained "Realpolitik." This, which was apparent to his contemporaries from the start of the war, has been clarified by one of the most painstaking biographers of Woodrow Wilson, Professor Arthur S. Link, who, with the benefit of forty years of hindsight, pointed out that at the start of World War I the formation and implementation of American foreign policy were in the hands of two men, Woodrow Wilson and William Jennings Bryan, both of whom were poorly equipped by background and training to manage the foreign relations of a great power. "They knew next to nothing about the administration of foreign affairs," Mr. Link wrote in the second volume of his well-documented biography of Wilson, "and were equally ignorant of the foreign policies of the other powers and of the tensions that imperiled the peace of the world in 1913 and 1914. . . . The seriousness of Wilson's and Bryan's ignorance of the techniques and issues of foreign affairs was heightened by the absence, a few months after Wilson's inauguration, of a strong bureaucracy capable of formulating and guiding foreign policy in an orderly way"—an absence, be it noted, owing to the wholesale replacement of trained diplomats by political hacks. But let Mr. Link resume:

> The most important weakness of New Freedom diplomacy, however, was the naiveté of its underlying assumption. Wilson and Bryan assumed that moral force controlled the relations of powers, that reason would prevail over ignorance and passion in the formation of public opinion, and that men and nations everywhere were automatically progressing towards an orderly and righteous international society. . . . New Freedom diplomacy failed in part, therefore, not because it was ignobly conceived, but because it ignored some of the basic facts of life. The truth was that not even idealists like Wilson and Bryan, or the allegedly idealistic American people, could live up to New Freedom ideals, and crises and contradictions arose one after another when apparent altruism had failed. Unhappily this failure was often due to the fact that American policy in the first instance had been based on the assumption that altruism was enough.[3]

Which is another way of saying that the nation's leaders during this great crisis had only a vague idea of what was happening in the world, knew nothing of its moving causes, lacked knowledge and background with which to appraise America's interests, and smugly identified inaction with righteousness and a benign pharisaism with wisdom.

For the first few weeks of the war TR made no public comment. When he spoke it was to give assent to America's policy of neutrality. Not until after he had talked with a committee of Belgians on September 27 did he begin to take a strong position in public on behalf of protesting the violation of Belgian neutrality, although as early as August 22, in a letter to his English friend Arthur Lee he said:

> I do not know whether I would be acting right if I were President or not, but it seems to me that if I were President I should register a very emphatic protest, a protest that would mean something against the levy of the huge war contributions upon Belgium. As regards

Belgium there is not even room for an argument. The Germans to suit their own purposes trampled on their solemn obligations to Belgium and on Belgium's rights. The Belgians have fought for their hearthstones and homes, and for the elemental rights without which it is not worthwhile to exist. . . . Even from the standpoint of brutal self-interest I think that Germany's invasion of Belgium was a mistake. The Germans, as I happen to know, counted confidently upon being mobilized within ten days, and at the end of that time having an army which had marched through Belgium break up the French before their mobilization was complete.[4]

In reply to a letter from the German propagandist and professor of philosophy at Harvard, Hugo Muensterberg, TR wrote with respect to Belgium: "The more I have studied the case the more keenly I have felt that there can be no satisfactory peace until Belgium's wrongs are redressed and until there is some kind of effective guarantee against a repetition of them as against her and others."[5] He then went on to consider the possibility of a German victory and said that "if Germany won this war, smashed the English fleet and destroyed the British empire, within a year or two she would insist upon taking the dominant position in South and Central America, and upon treating the United States precisely as she treated Japan when she joined with Russia and France against Japan twenty years ago and took Kiau-Chow as her share."[6]

TR's relative silence during these first months has puzzled both friends and critics. To me the logical explanation is that he knew the gravity of the crisis; that the responsibility for meeting it was Wilson's, not TR's; that the more he disagreed with the administration the more he felt it was incumbent on him as former president to refrain as long as possible from publicly criticizing it during this crucial period in the nation's history. Furthermore, even though he knew that the Secretary of State was happily ignorant of world affairs and was useless to the President, he knew that Mr. Wilson might—and certainly should—have access to sources of reliable information that TR lacked.

These sources should have been other than the American ambassadors and ministers in the principal European capitals at the outbreak of the war, of whom only Walter Hines Page in London could be regarded as a man with an enlightened grasp of world affairs, and only Myron T. Herrick in Paris had served long enough to have learned something about the country to which he was accredited. But what TR did not know then was that Mr. Wilson shunned advice and had an aversion to persons reputed to be experts in particular fields. In other words the President was evaluating a world crisis in a vacuum, alone with his typewriter.

In spite of this, Mr. Roosevelt refrained from public criticism. When, in January, 1915, he put in book form the articles that he had written for *The New York Times*, *Outlook*, and *Metropolitan Magazine* after the war had started, he amplified the idea that "in facing a difficult and critical situation any administration is entitled to a free hand until it has had time to develop the action which it considers appropriate." He added that he "kept silence as long as silence was compatible with regard for the national honor and welfare," and explained that "it has become evident that the administration has had no plan whatever save the dexterous avoidance of all responsibility and therefore all duty, and the effort to persuade our people as a whole that this inaction is for their interest—combined with other less openly expressed and less worthy efforts of a purely political type." He then went on to charge that if President Wilson and Secretary Bryan "had been thoroughly acquainted in advance, as of course they ought to have been acquainted, with the European situation, and if they had possessed an intelligent and resolute purpose squarely to meet their heavy responsibilities . . . they would have taken action on July 29th, 30th or 31st, certainly not later than August 1st."[7] In a letter to his close friend and one-time protégé, Henry L. Stimson, TR later blamed himself for having stated a month after the start of the war that we had no responsibility for Belgium. But he added that "I was wrong in following the President for the first sixty days; and all that can be said in my favor is that even though it was sixty days before I abandoned the idea of supporting the President and took my own line on Americanism, International Duty and Preparedness, yet it was a year and a quarter later before the other men of my class in politics began to follow me."[8]

To contend that Mr. Wilson lacked a strong feeling of obligation to do the best for the country in this great crisis would be unjust. His eagerness to keep the United States out of the war reflected the determination of the overwhelming mass of the American people. Like them he believed that the country could and should keep out. The obvious technical procedure was to declare and implement America's neutrality. This accorded with traditional American policy, dating from Washington's proclamation of neutrality in 1793. During and after the Napoleonic wars a body of international legal postulates about neutrality had been discussed in diplomatic notes and at international conferences, but there had never been accord among the powers as to just how neutral "rights" might be defined, nor what was to be done when and if a belligerent ignored them. There had long been, in fact, a basic conflict about neutral "rights" between diplomats and military men, regardless of nationality—a conflict that even reached into the ranks of the German High Command during World War I, centering, in particular, on submarine warfare.

Without going into the details of the complex subject of neutrality a few simple guidelines may be postulated:

1) However vigorously neutrals may insist that their non-belligerent status entitles them to certain "rights" (most of which center on commerce in time of war), these rights are only maintainable so long as the belligerents are willing to concede them. In other words neutral rights, even if set forth in diplomatic declarations, are not embodied in binding treaties and agreements

that can be enforced by neutrals in the face of belligerent opposition. In practice belligerents have regarded neutral rights as restrictions on their freedom of belligerency, and as belligerency is by implication lawless—or at least contemptuous of restraints of any kind—belligerents have tended to disregard the demands and contentions of neutrals with respect to neutral "rights" whenever they have felt that to do so was in their interest—i.e., that defiance of neutral rights would not bring reprisals on a belligerent that might adversely affect its chances of victory.

2) From this it follows that the likelihood that a neutral can maintain its rights depends on the extent to which these rights conflict with the interests of a belligerent. The decision rests with the belligerent, regardless of the eagerness of a neutral to see its rights upheld.

3) The inescapable conclusion is that if a belligerent believes that it will be deprived of victory or will find the winning of the war more difficult if it agrees to maintain a right claimed by a neutral, the belligerent will either evade complying with that right or will openly flout it. The determining factor in a belligerent's decision will be how much damage a neutral can inflict on the belligerent in the form of reprisals. Will the neutral stop short of war, such as confiscation of the belligerent's shipping in neutral ports? Will the neutral fight? If it fights, can it bring effective military pressure to bear in a short enough time to affect adversely the offending belligerent's expectation or hope of winning the war? In other words what is the potential effective power of a neutral nation? If the neutral goes to war, how may this influence the military outcome? What potential side issues exist, such as encouraging other neutrals to enter the war against the offending belligerent?

The answers to these questions depend on strategy and expedience, rather than on juridical factors. Yet the evidence is overwhelming that Wilson's primary if not exclusive concern was with theory and legality. He apparently thought that rigid adherence to the principles of neutrality as developed during the preceding century would effectively keep the United States out of war. Viewed purely abstractly the theoretical argument was in Wilson's favor. But this theory ignored the fact that in a world at war eventualities could arise abroad that would leave the American government no alternative but to act counter to previously expressed popular opinion. In other words the President as executor and implementor of public opinion that favored strict neutrality might find himself in opposition to the President as commander-in-chief of the army and navy—as, in fact, happened when Germany developed the submarine campaign against neutral (including American) shipping. The decision to blockade Britain was made by the German High Command with a view to Germany's military needs without regard to the wishes of the American people. Yet this German decision had enormous repercussions on the development of American policy, regardless of American public opinion. When the German government decided on unrestricted submarine warfare against Allied and neutral commercial vessels, which was announced effective as of February 1, 1917, the German High Command took into consideration the possibility that this policy might lead to an open break with the government of the United States, but concluded that even if America went to war it could not prevent a German victory.

I happened to be in Spain at the time and remember reading in a Spanish newspaper an interview with either Grand Admiral von Tirpitz or some other well-known spokesman for the German High Command, which, in summary, explained that the United States did not have an army large enough to influence the outcome of the war; that even if it were to raise one, it could not train it in time; that even if it could train it this army could not be adequately armed; that even if armed, it could not be transported in sufficient numbers in time to prevent a German victory. Therefore even if the German decision led to a declaration of war by the United States, Germany had nothing to lose or even to fear from such an eventuality. The German High Command was convinced that Germany would win the war before the United States could become a dangerous adversary.

Most of President Wilson's supporters believed not only that we should, but that we could, keep out of war. They felt that a policy of strict neutrality would place the United States in the position of being able to act as arbiter between the two contending sides, and they did not want to see the President take any action that would cripple his potentialities as a peacemaker. Apart from the fact that the role of mediator attracted him, the eagerness to keep the country out of war was reinforced by his conviction that the function of a President is to follow, not to guide, public opinion, and he knew that the mass of the American people wanted to keep the United States out of war. He appears to have had few doubts that rigid adherence to the principles of neutrality as developed during the preceding century could attain this objective. In fact, he looked on neutrality as a substitute for preparedness, unaware that neutrality, to be effective, must be based on armed might. As one of his biographers[9] put it "he simply was not willing to pay the political and social costs of effective preparation for a war that might not, after all, occur."

TR, in contrast, not only believed in strengthening the nation's armed forces but believed that one of the main functions of the President was to mold and lead public opinion. He acted on the assumption that the mass of the American people had neither the knowledge, the interest, nor the time to formulate sound judgments on such complicated problems of policy as foreign affairs, and that, in consequence, the responsibility for determining foreign policy rested on the President and his advisers. When he needed congressional support for a foreign policy decision he took the lead in stirring it up. Mr. Wilson, in contrast, was inclined to do little to influence congressional leaders to support his policies. His relations with Congress, never happy or very successful, made him in this field as in the formulation of public opinion more of a follower than a leader.

On February 4, 1915, the German government announced that a submarine blockade of Great Britain would begin on February 18. The American government replied under date of February 10, warning the German government that it would hold that government to a "strict accountability"—a phrase which, while as broad as the seas around Britain, was a diplomatic warning that serious consequences might follow, such as the breaking off of diplomatic relations or even war. But with his characteristic fondness for verbal obfuscation Mr. Wilson refrained from directly challenging the submarine campaign. In March and April of 1915, as Wilson's biographer, A. S. Link put it[10] the conviction gradually spread in Germany that the American government had no intention of enforcing its threats. "In the German view, Bernstorff's messages from Washington gave proof positive that the disdain now spreading in Berlin was justified. 'The policy of the American government,' he reported . . . 'is dominated by the one thought of not becoming involved in any complication whatever. "*We want to stay out of everything*" is the single rule. . . . The government here is continually attempting to squirm out of every problem without getting into severe difficulties.' "

On May 7 the *Lusitania* was sunk, with a loss of 1,198 lives, including 124 Americans. I was in London on a week's leave from the American Embassy in Paris. On the afternoon of May 7 I had had tea with Lord Bryce, author of *The American Commonwealth*. Walking back to Garland's Hotel I passed a news vendor. In those days news vendors displayed posters listing the main story of the day. His had on it in large capitals two words: "Lusitania Sunk!" From a letter written to my mother two days later I quote: "This thing hit me as, I believe nothing in my whole life ever has. It has knocked the bottom out of me. When I first read it . . . I found myself saying: 'I won't believe it. It can't be true. It isn't possible. I won't believe it!' But I hurried to the Cunard office." In the diary I find: "There I saw a sign saying that the vessel had been torpedoed and sunk. I merely gulped and hurried out into the street, where I stood dazed and stunned, and then walked back to the hotel, trying my best not to lose control of myself." I went back several times that night to the Cunard office, but the list of survivors was slow in being compiled, owing no doubt to the physical difficulty of assembling and checking information.

We at the embassy in Paris had been trying—not very successfully—to follow President Wilson's injunction to be "neutral in thought as well as in deed." But the *Lusitania* turned us overnight into bitter anti-Germans. Not only the extreme barbarity of the act, but the obvious implication that the United States might postpone, but could not evade, being drawn into the war, thenceforth colored all our reactions. I could not, of course, as a twenty-two-year-old neophyte in the foreign service, foresee just what would happen or when. But I knew—rightly—that the end of an era had come and that because of this barbarous and inhumane act the secure, orderly way of life into which I had been born was doomed. It was just a question of time before we would be in the war, and I knew that I, the least martial and bellicose of all my Roosevelt contemporaries, would have to join the army.

My reaction was obviously personalized—as was inevitable in a normally self-centered youngster. Equally naturally, the reaction of TR, when called to the telephone in the middle of the night by one of the press associations and asked for a statement, was that of a statesman and historian profoundly shocked by an incident that was sure to loom large in the development of world affairs. "This represents not merely piracy," he said, "but piracy on a vaster scale of murder than old-time pirates ever practiced. . . . It is warfare against innocent men, women and children, travelling on the ocean, and our own fellow-countrymen and countrywomen, who are among the sufferers. It seems inconceivable that we can refrain from taking action in this matter, for we owe it not only to humanity but to our own self-respect."[11] The day before the sinking, as I have already indicated, he had written to "Cal" O'Laughlin that if he were President he would warn the German government that if the *Lusitania* were sunk and Americans lost their lives, he would confiscate all the German interned ships. At about the same time he told my mother that if he had been in the White House when the warning from the German Embassy appeared he would have given Bernstorff, the German ambassador, his passport and placed him on the *Lusitania*. While this statement was probably made after the event, it is sufficiently characteristic of his way of acting to suggest that he would have done something very much like it.

Arthur S. Link's meticulous biography of Wilson gives a vivid picture of Wilson's reaction to the *Lusitania* incident. That the President was deeply distressed is obvious. But for three days he cut himself off from everyone, with the exception of his private secretary, Joseph P. Tumulty, and had no contact with the Secretary of State or anyone else in the Department. As Mr. Link put it, he deliberately sought "to set an example of calmness and detachment for his people in this time of stress."[12] During these three days, he brooded over what he should do and drafted a note to the German government. It must have been a harrowing three days of self-imposed loneliness and soul-searching, and led (I quote once more from Professor Link) to "an appeal on the high ground of humanity to the German government to abandon its entire submarine campaign against commerce."[13] Before, even, he had finished drafting his note he made his first public statement. This was to a group of newly naturalized citizens in Convention Hall in Philadelphia, in which, although without direct reference to the *Lusitania*, he said: "The example of America must be the example not merely of peace because it will not fight, but of peace because peace is the healing and elevating influence of the world and strife is not. There is such a thing as a man being too proud to fight. There is such a thing as a nation being so right that it does not need to convince others by force that it is right."[14]

Even though this statement did not undermine the effectiveness of the note to Germany as much as would a proposed press release that Wilson first agreed to issue and then withdrew, it certainly encouraged the German government to think or hope that President Wilson did not really mean what he said in his note. The German foreign office's conclusion that this was the correct interpretation of the first *Lusitania* note was reinforced when the Austrian ambassador to the United States, Konstantin Dumba, reported to Vienna for transmission to the German government that Secretary Bryan had told him that the *Lusitania* note "had to be written in a much sharper form than the one sent to England on March 30, but that nevertheless, it was intended in a friendly manner and he (Bryan) hopes for an answer in the same friendly tone and spirit."[15] In diplomatic procedure this was tantamount to saying that the note need not be regarded too seriously. Had Mr. Wilson taken counsel with any trained diplomat or other expert in the conduct of foreign relations he would unquestionably have been told that it would be interpreted in this manner. But by deliberately cutting himself off from all advisers he deprived himself of the advice of men experienced in the ways of world politics at a time when he sorely needed it.

15

HIS FINEST HOURS

ALTHOUGH I RECEIVED numerous letters and books from TR while I worked at the American Embassy in Paris, I did not see him again until the spring of 1916 when I returned to Oyster Bay. Since the autumn of 1914 he had been deep in his campaign to arouse the nation to the need of military and naval preparedness, and when I asked him for background material he gave me two volumes, a recently published biographical sketch of him by his friend and classmate Charles G. Washburn and Frederick Scott Oliver's *Ordeal by Battle*. In the former he wrote under date of April 19, 1916: "Dear Nick, see pp. 105-108. Your aff cousin Theodore Roosevelt." These pages contain extracts from his special message to Congress, dated April 14, 1908, about the need for modernizing and strengthening the navy. In this message appear familiar phrases:

It is mischievous folly for any statesman to assume that this world has yet reached the stage when a proud nation, jealous of its honor and conscious of its great mission in the world, can be content to rely for peace upon the forbearance of other powers. . . . Events still fresh in the mind of every thinking man show that neither arbitration nor any other device can as yet be invoked to prevent the gravest and most terrible wrongdoing to peoples who are either few in numbers or who, if numerous, have lost the first and most important of national virtues—the capacity for self-defense. . . . If we desire to secure peace it must be known that we are at all times ready for war.[1]

Three years earlier he had written his friend Spring-Rice: "My object is to keep America in trim so that fighting her shall be too expensive and dangerous a task to likely be undertaken by anybody."[2] His underlying philosophy was well phrased in the twenty-first verse of the eleventh chapter of the Gospel according to St. Luke, which he often quoted during the years 1914–1917: "When a strong man armed keepeth his palace, his goods are in peace."

Frederick Scott Oliver's book was a brilliant analysis of the events leading up to the First World War, with particular stress on a simple premise: "This war was not inevitable; it could have been avoided, but on one condition—*if England had been prepared.*"[3] By way of emphasizing the importance of Britain's unpreparedness Oliver explained:

> Our armament did not correspond with our policy. It was clear that they [the government] would not be able to uphold that policy if it were put to the supreme test of war. It was impossible to abandon our policy. It was not impossible—and it was not in 1912 too late—to set about strengthening our armaments. Nothing of the kind, however, was undertaken by the government, whose spokesmen, official and unofficial, employed themselves more congenially in deriding and rebuking Lord Roberts for calling attention to the dangers.[4]
>
> [Field Marshall Lord Roberts had become in the years of his retirement the main spokesman of the advocates of military preparedness to meet the impending challenge of German navalism and militarism.]

Oliver's discussion of the attitude of the British government as the world war approached has a familiar ring to Americans who remember the years 1914–1917 in this country. He pointed out that it was absurd to suppose that the government

> could have failed to realize the extent of the danger, or our unpreparedness to meet it, unless they had purposely buried their heads in the sand. They knew that they had not a big enough army, and that this fact might ruin their whole policy. Why did they never say so?

Why, when Lord Roberts said so, did they treat him with contumely, and make every effort to discredit him? Why was nothing done by them during their whole period of office to increase the army and thereby diminish the numerical superiority of their adversaries? On the contrary, they actually reduced the army, assuring the country that they had no use for so many trained soldiers. Moreover, the timidity or secretiveness of the Government prevented England from having what is worth several army corps, and what proved the salvation of France—a National Policy, fully agreed and appealing to the hearts and consciences of the whole people.[5]

To which he added his original refrain in a different form: "When a country is fully prepared it can afford to wait and see if there will be a war; but not otherwise."[6] And again: "If England had possessed such an army as would have enabled her to intervene with effect in European affairs, she would almost certainly never have been called upon to intervene."[7]

Oliver, of course, was not alone in stressing the close interrelationships between policy and armament. The principle applied to neutrals as much as—or perhaps even more than—it applied to belligerents, because a nation either contemplating or fearing war almost always prepared for offensive or defensive action. Neutrals, in contrast, usually lulled themselves into the false security of good intentions. But for reasons that, as far as I know, have not yet been clearly set forth, President Wilson, an ardent devotee of neutrality, was not only hostile but resistant to all calls for military and naval preparedness in the first ten months of the war. In a footnote in his biography of Wilson, Professor Link remarks that on October 19, 1914, "Wilson laughingly referred to the discussion over preparedness as 'good mental exercise,' adding that talk of this kind had been going on ever since he was a boy of ten.' (Source, *N. Y. Times,* Oct. 20, 1914) Again on November 30, 1914, he referred to the movement for a special Congressional investigation [of the state of the nation's defenses] as 'untimely.' (id. Dec. 1, 1914)" In his annual message on December 8, 1914, the President stated that "we shall not alter our attitude . . . because some amongst us are nervous or excited," and he went on to say that a change of policy "would mean merely that we had lost our self-possession, that we had been thrown off our balance by a war with which we had nothing to do, whose causes cannot touch us, whose very existence affords us opportunities of friendship and disinterested service which should make us ashamed of any thought of hostility or fearful preparation for trouble."[8] TR, referring in his volume, *America and the World War*, to another part of the same message called attention to the President's remarks on the disagreement among experts as to whether and how the navy should be increased, and, in particular, to Mr. Wilson's interjection: "I turn away from the subject. It is not new. There is no new need to discuss it." To which TR wryly remarked that he was reminded of Chapter XI of *Our Mutual Friend* by Charles Dickens, in which Mr. Podsnap referred to "getting rid of disagreeables" by the use of the phrases: "I don't want to know about them! I don't admit them!" thus clearing the world of its most difficult problems by sweeping them behind him. It was not until September, 1915, four months after the sinking of the *Lusitania*, that, in response to increasing public clamor for preparedness, Mr. Wilson dropped his opposition to it, although with obvious misgivings and without embracing a program of preparedness that approached the demands of the advocates of adequate national defenses. The President knew perhaps better than his critics how little enthusiasm there was in Congress for any kind of preparedness at that time, but he had shown little inclination to try to arouse Congress to support preparedness.

Still later in the same volume TR referred to Bryan's remarks about the preparedness campaign: "The President knows that if this country needed a million men, and needed them in a day, the call would go out at sunrise and the sun would go down on a million men in arms." This reminded TR of a Bryanite senator who went even further than Mr. Bryan by saying that in the event of war "ten million freemen would spring to arms, the equals of any regular soldiers in the world." But, as TR pointed out, these ten million men would have "at the outside four hundred thousand modern rifles to which to spring. Perhaps six hundred thousand more could spring to squirrel pieces and fairly good shotguns. The remaining nine million would have to 'spring' to axes, scythes, handsaws, gimlets and similar arms." In retrospect it is not surprising that, to repeat Mr. Wilson's words, "some amongst us are nervous or excited."

The bare record of the government's expenditure on the army and navy gives a clear idea of the administration's interest in preparedness. In the fiscal year ending June 30, 1915, the federal government spent six million dollars less on the army than it had during the year ending June 30, 1914. In the year ending June 30, 1916, the expenditures for the army had been still further cut by seventeen million dollars. Corresponding expenditures for the navy increased about two million for the fiscal year ending June 30, 1915, over the year 1914, and expenditures during the year ending June 30, 1916, were up about twelve million dollars, or approximately 7 per cent, over those in the previous year. In other words despite the increasing evidences of the need for building up the nation's defenses practically nothing was done.[9] The United States declared war on April 6, 1917, and by the end of the then current fiscal year (i.e., June 30, 1917) army expenditures had approximately doubled and those for the navy had increased by about a quarter. This reflected America's entry into the war. It was a start, but as woefully belated as it was inadequate.

As TR kept insisting, the important thing was to be wise in time. As he put it in an article published in late 1914: "from the moment when war was declared, it became inexcusable of the administration not to take immediate steps to put the navy into efficient shape, and at least to make our military forces on land more respectable."[10] A year later, while Wilson had continued to drag his feet on preparedness, TR wrote: "Never in the country's history has there been a more stupendous instance of folly than this crowning folly of waiting eighteen months after the elemental clash of nations took place before even making a start in an effort—and an utterly inefficient and insufficient effort—for some kind of preparation to ward off disaster in the future."[11] Coupling the President's unwillingness to embark on a sound plan of military preparedness with his remarks after the sinking of the *Lusitania* about being too proud to fight, TR resorted to the devastating technique of a theoretical analogy: "If after the firing on Sumter, Lincoln had immediately in a speech declared that friends of the union might be 'too proud to fight' and had spent the next four months exchanging 'firm' diplomatic notes with Jefferson Davis, he would have received the enthusiastic support of ardent adherents of peace—and we would have had no country."[12] Later in the same volume TR used a phrase reminiscent of his friend Frederick Scott Oliver: "The prime and all-important lesson to learn is that while preparedness will not guarantee a nation against war, unpreparedness eventually insures not merely war, but utter disaster."[13]

In spite of the fact that at the outbreak of the war TR was at the lowest ebb of his popularity and influence—and it should be remembered that no former President five years out of office is looked up to as a popular leader—the vigor and obvious sincerity of his espousal of the cause of preparedness aroused increasing interest and approval. It is probably no exaggeration to say that in the autumn of 1914 ninety-nine out of every hundred Americans sincerely believed that the war was no concern of theirs, directly or indirectly and hoped that nothing could or would drag the United States into the conflict. But TR not only felt very strongly about the need of preparedness for the United States as a neutral, but also became increasingly concerned about the danger to the United States of a German victory. On both counts he believed in the importance of preparing, and the "preacher militant" in him compelled him to lead the cause.

Fortunately he had a vigorous ally and supporter in Major General Leonard Wood, his old associate in the Rough Riders. The general had completed his tour of duty as Chief of Staff in 1913, during which, among other achievements, he had interested a number of colleges in the country in instituting reserve officers' training camps in which a select number of undergraduates would receive indoctrination in the elements of military service. Out of this grew what came to be known as the "Plattsburg movement," in which selected civilians ranging from college undergraduates to men in their fifties received a four weeks' course of elementary military training under thoroughly capable West Point graduates—little enough at best, but better than nothing.

It was the nation's good fortune that in these antipreparedness days no one close to Wilson was percipient enough to foresee the value and ultimate popularity of these officers' training camps. Otherwise the fact that the camps had been organized and pushed by General Wood and strongly supported by Theodore Roosevelt and that among those who attended the first Plattsburg Camp in 1915 were such outstanding Republicans as Robert Bacon, formerly Secretary of State, and Henry L. Stimson, formerly Secretary of War, would almost surely have turned the partisan-minded administration against them. Attendance in 1915 was approximately twelve hundred at Plattsburg, and another five hundred at Monterey, on the West Coast. The next year the numbers had increased nearly tenfold, and the graduates of these camps formed a steadily growing army of advocates of military preparedness. Theodore Roosevelt, who strongly supported the movement and whose sons and relatives attended the camps, could be attacked but not muzzled. General Wood, however, was rebuked by the Secretary of War at the direction of the President for having permitted, with the approval of the War Department, Theodore Roosevelt to address the Plattsburg Camp. Fortunately the general was not prevented from continuing his active support of the camps. In fact, he continued to speak in behalf of preparedness on all possible occasions, stressing such elemental factors as the impossibility of improvising weapons; the time required to train officers; the need for long-range planning for the equipping and moving of men. At a hearing before the Senate Committee on Military Affairs on January 18, 1916, he decried the folly of "leaving the burden of war to the time of war. . . . The burden of war must be spread over a very much longer time than the period of war. This burden must be in the form of preparation, organization, provision of supplies, training of men, etc., all with the object of making the war short, successful; and its burden as light as possible."[14] How right General Wood was may be judged from the fact that it was over a year from the date of our entry into the First World War before we were able to place four divisions in the line of battle—a delay owing as much to lack of equipment as to lack of training and of over-all preparedness.[15]

As late as January 31, 1917, General Wood, appearing again before the Senate Committee on Military Affairs, reverted again to the deplorable lack of supplies of all kinds: "We stand practically as unprepared as when the great war began," he explained, "and are apparently unobservant of its clear lessons and unappreciative of the fact that no amount of money and no amount of effort can purchase time or make good its loss. Whatever the ultimate organizations of our resources may be, there is no question whatever as to the necessity for supplying a sufficiency of the above equipment, arms and munitions to promptly equip and arm a force of at least two and a half million volunteers with adequate reserves for a year."[16] Both he and TR were fighting an uphill fight against an administration that, like the government of Britain in the year or two before the start of the war, had deliberately refused to face the shape of the inevitable.

TR's bitterness against Wilson for dragging his feet about preparedness in a sense epitomizes the fundamental difference in the mental processes of the two men. TR, as has been made abundantly clear, was keenly aware of the realities of world politics. He was convinced that American participation, given the policies that Wilson was following, was unavoidable. The question was not whether, but how soon, we would become involved—as we ultimately did. He knew that every month's delay in facing the unavoidable—or perhaps it should be called the inescapable—involvement meant an increase in the destruction of human lives and property. It was obvious that the increasing exhaustion of the Allied nations meant that there would be increasing demands on the United States for men and assistance. From this the conclusion was clear—that the sooner the United States entered the war the sooner the war would end, provided the United States availed itself of its opportunity to speed up its armaments of all kinds, to substitute machine guns and howitzers for handsaws and scythes. The addition of America's war potential to the resources of the Allied powers would mean that victory for Germany would be impossible. In contrast, Wilson's policy of attenuated abstention could not keep us out of war and would surely cost America more lives and other sacrifices than would early intervention.

The speculative judgment made in 1964 by one of America's well-known historians, Samuel Eliot Morison, that it might have been best if the United States had entered the war earlier, confirms TR's position at the time: "Had she been able to bring her strength to bear in 1916," the professor wrote in his *Oxford History of the United States,* "the war would probably have been over within a year, [and] the disastrous loss of life and breakdown of civilized standards would have ended two years earlier than it did. . . ."[17] The fact that Professor Morison is a leading authority on strategy as well as on history lends special pertinence to his estimate.

The clearness with which TR saw the futility and folly of Wilson's policy of unconscionable delay surely was a major factor in intensifying the bitterness that he felt for Wilson. But to apply the word *hatred* to TR's attitude, as numerous historians have done, is a misreading of his character. Deep resentment, open contempt for Wilson's refusal to face the inescapable, profound bitterness at the realization of what American manhood would pay because of Wilson's policy—all these, I am sure, were ever present in TR's thinking about the war. But hate—certainly in the meaning of the word as defined in the Oxford dictionary—does not strike me as accurate: "an emotion of extreme dislike or aversion, detestation, abhorrence, hatred"—which last word is further defined as "enmity, ill-will, malevolence." TR was profoundly upset about what Wilson was doing to the country and to the American people. His bitterness was not based on personal grounds. Certainly there was in it no malevolence or ill-will. Rather it was a deeply felt scorn for a policy with respect to the warring nations, which, in the light of his own experience and knowledge, TR was convinced was disastrous. Obviously when the autumn of 1916 came round his contempt was heightened by the cynicism of the campaign slogan that played such a large part in the reelection of Wilson in 1916—"He kept us out of war"—a slogan that TR knew was either intended to deceive by implying that only through keeping Wilson in office would the United States keep out of war or was the product of such fatuous blindness that it was a grim reflection on the intelligence and integrity of the leading candidate for the great office of President of the United States.

When, a few weeks after the election, President Wilson finally realized that American participation in the war was no longer avoidable, he carried over into the preparation for war the highly personalized approach that had hitherto shaped his thinking. The case of Henry L. Stimson is illuminating. This distinguished citizen who had been Secretary of War in Taft's cabinet and who later served as Secretary of State under President Hoover and again as Secretary of War under FDR, joined the army in the summer of 1917 and was assigned to the War College, where he worked as a staff intelligence officer, drilled with the artillery at Fort Myer, and in the evenings studied the duties of artillery officers with the hope of being assigned for duty overseas. As the field artillery was expanding rapidly and there was a great shortage of officers, especially for such ranks as lieutenant-colonel and colonel, his name was placed on a list of officers recommended for promotion to lieutenant-colonel and assignment to field service. It was removed from this list by Newton D. Baker, then Secretary of War. When Stimson protested to Baker, the latter told him that he did not want the army used as a source of glory for politicians. There is nothing in the record to show that Baker had acted at Wilson's direction, but there can be little doubt that the sentiment which he expressed reflected Wilson's own views—especially if the politicians happened to be Republicans. Baker subsequently withdrew his objection to the promotion of the former Secretary of War to a relatively minor, completely nonpolitical post, apparently on the urging of Major General Hugh L. Scott, the Chief of Staff.[18]

While many persons believed that President Wilson's rejection of TR's offer to raise a division and accompany it to France was based on his resentment of TR's scathing criticism of the President during the first two years of the war, it is only fair to Wilson to point out that whatever his emotional resistance to TR's offer, there were numerous strong arguments against the proposal. To begin with, while I do not have any notes to verify the item, and, as yet (January, 1967) Professor Link's volume on Wilson that would throw light on the subject has not been published, I think it would be an intelligent guess that General Pershing, who was slated to be Commander-in-Chief of the American Expeditionary Force, was opposed to TR's project. Pershing was a good—but not a great—officer, a man of integrity and good sense, rigid but fair, with the traditional West Pointer's disdain for nonprofessional soldiers. Many West Pointers, even including admirers of TR, disapproved of TR's project for at least four reasons: 1) It would inject a unit of volunteers into an army that would otherwise be manned entirely by draftees. 2) It would be delegating as a junior general officer a man whose major training had been that of a top commander. 3) It would be placing in high military office a non-West Pointer. 4) It would inject into the high command a figure with a fatal attraction for the press and with countless friends among newspapermen, who would look to him for news about events or conditions that the Commander-in-Chief might prefer to see passed over unnoticed. In addition to which General Pershing may well have considered a more personal reason—that, given his own opposition to TR's proposal, he sensed that it could strengthen his relations with the President if he advocated a course that he knew would bring smug satisfaction to Mr. Wilson's unforgiving soul. By this I do not mean to imply that Pershing's decision was affected by Wilson's prejudices but only that, feeling that the project deserved to be rejected, he was not averse to acquiring merit in Wilson's eyes by rejecting a plan which the President disapproved.

As a matter of fact there were even greater latent complications. The foremost of these was the extraordinary admiration that so many Europeans had for TR, and the fact that throughout Europe a half-century ago a man who had held high office—who had been President, or prime minister, or foreign secretary—was regarded as still having influence over the office that he had held. Foreign leaders would almost surely appeal to TR to influence Woodrow Wilson, without realizing that were TR to attempt to do so he would be met with unyielding resistance. Were TR to fail to try, he would arouse the resentment of those attempting to use him. Furthermore, TR numbered among his close friends countless Europeans in high office—men who believed in him and confided in him, from whom he might learn things not known in Washington. Inevitably the eagerness of European leaders to receive this brigadier general would have aroused resentment and jealousy on the part of generals of higher rank and would have encouraged eager suspicions and misunderstandings in the White House and the War Department.

Furthermore, it was all very well for TR to ask only for command of a single brigade in the division, but the division would be subject to orders of General Pershing or one of his representatives—and even those who admired and loved TR found it hard to visualize him in the role of a subordinate. He never shirked responsibility—in fact, he reached out to grasp it; he was impatient and had a passion for getting things done; he did not suffer blunderers gladly. His self-confidence had become deeply ingrained, and as he was beyond fear and had no personal ambition other than to do a good job, he was beyond restraint. Major General James G. Harbord, a devoted admirer of TR and a keen judge of men, summed it up by saying: "How good a subordinate he would have made after nearly eight years as commander in chief; how well his aggressive, dominating personality would have fitted into the difficult diplomatic situation in which the patient tact of General Pershing was strained to the utmost, only Divine Omniscience can know."[19] TR's request to raise a division was refused—just as later Leonard Wood was denied the right to go to France with the division that he had trained. Both men had publicly advocated military preparedness at a time when President Wilson opposed it. The fact that their interpretation of the world situation had been correct did not endear them to the mistaken President. Both accepted their intended humiliation with dignity and turned to other ways in which to serve their country in this great crisis, the colonel proudly sending his four sons to war, the general continuing in the task of training recruits and aspirant officers with unremitting skill and cheerfulness. I was to see much of General Wood in the years to come —I served as his secretary throughout the 1920 campaign for the Republican nomination for the presidency and in 1926 spent a part of the winter with him when he was Governor General of the Philippines—and formed a high regard for his character. Like TR he radiated integrity, courage, and good humor. Both men could—and should—have been given positions of outstanding importance in winning the war, but both were denied active service at the front.

In a world that has survived two global wars and faces possible extinction in a third, TR's eagerness to be a soldier may seem puzzling. Because his service with the Rough Riders played a dramatic role in shaping his subsequent career, there are those who assume that his prime motive in going to war was to seek nationwide notoriety. He may well have hoped—or dreamed—that he would have a distinguished military career. He knew that he had unusual gifts of leadership, and therefore would probably be a good officer of volunteers—as, in fact, he was. But glory—if any—would be only incidental. His compelling motive in seeking active service was, I am sure, a strong sense of duty. Not only did he accept the obligation to serve his country in time of war, but he was convinced that those who, like himself, publicly supported policies leading to war were morally obligated to take an active part in the war they advocated. Put in even simpler terms, he was ready to risk his life in support of a course of action that he had urged on his fellow countrymen. His views on this are made clear in letters written as the crisis with Spain came to a head in 1898.

To deduce from his advocacy of war with Spain and, later, with Germany that he was a "jingo" and a "warmonger" is to ignore the all-important fact that in his day and for generations before him war was an accepted means of implementing national policy. The history of the last four centuries contains numerous instances of war waged in the pursuit of national policy. In the early nineteenth century Napoleon Bonaparte had built a continental empire by war—and was overthrown by war. In 1870 the new German Empire was consolidated by war, and forty-four years later sought world domination by war. It was wiped out in 1918 largely because of American military and financial assistance to Germany's enemies. The American nation had been cradled in war in the days of the revolution—and later was nearly destroyed by war between the states. Being essentially a pragmatist rather than a man of a speculative or philosophical turn of mind, TR was concerned with the world as he knew it, rather than with theories of how it could or should be improved, and the world that he knew not only accepted but glorified war. As I have noted elsewhere, he believed firmly the New Testament concept that when a strong man armed keepeth his palace his goods are in peace. I often heard him quote this proverb in driving home an argument in behalf of military preparedness.

There has been speculation that his own eagerness for active service not only in the war with Spain but in the First World War was somehow connected with supposed disappointment that his father, whom he worshiped, had not enlisted for military duty during the Civil War. I never heard him express his views on this, but knowing his strong sense of duty I doubt that his attitude about his own role in either war would have been different had his father seen active military service in the Civil War—unless his father's example would have still further strengthened his own determination to serve his country to the very best of his ability.

From the spring of 1917 into the summer of 1918 I was away from Oyster Bay, first at the Reserve Officers Training Camp at Fort Oglethorpe and then with the 322d Infantry of the 81st Division, which was trained at Camp Jackson, near Columbia, South Carolina. TR's four sons went abroad early and had distinguished military careers. He followed these careers with pride and intense interest and made it a point to inform the families of each son as to how the others were faring. One of his daughters-in-law told me that every single week he wrote a longhand letter to each of his daughters-in-law, reporting on matters of interest to her.

Came the afternoon of July 17, 1918. The correspondent of the Associated Press drove up to Sagamore Hill with an obviously garbled but equally obviously disturbing cable. Could TR make anything out of it? As he read it he realized that something must have happened to one of the boys. He knew that it couldn't be Theodore, Jr. who was in a hospital; or Archie, who was behind the lines recovering from wounds; or Kermit, who was not in a danger zone. Which meant it must be Quentin, who only a few days before had shot down his first German pilot. But it was far from clear what had happened. TR asked the AP man to go back and see what he could find out by cabling to Europe —and under no circumstances to say anything that might reach Mrs. Roosevelt. And without a sign of his own distress, he dressed for dinner and spent a quiet evening reading to her.

Early the next morning the AP man returned. One look at him and TR knew that Quentin was gone—the youngest, the gayest and most whimsical, and the most promising of them all. TR had known, of course, that this could happen—that even none of the sons might come back. His instant concern was for the boy's mother—and she, as I have already made clear, had much of the Spartan in her. It was only two or three weeks later that I went to Sagamore to say good-bye to them the day before my division sailed for Europe. I have described in Chapter III how the sight of me in uniform was, for a brief instant, more than Cousin Edith could bear, with all the associations of Archie and Quentin and myself as childhood playmates. She turned away for a second—and then both of them began asking me about the division and my part in it and when we were sailing—just as if nothing had happened. And yet a few days later TR wrote his daughter, Ethel Derby: "There is no use making believe that his death is other than a terrible and irretrievable calamity; nothing atones for it, but he has won a shining place as the embodiment in this war of the spirit of service and sacrifice of the nation."[20]

That was the last time I saw TR. When word of his death

came I was in Switzerland, en route to Austria to join TR's old friend Professor Archibald Cary Coolidge, who represented in Vienna the American Commission to Negotiate Peace. TR had two long sieges in the hospital in the autumn and early winter but had returned to Sagamore for Christmas and seemed to be picking up. On January 5, 1919, he dictated letters and wrote a piece for the *Kansas City Star*, to which he was then a regular contributor. He had had a happy day—as happy as any day could be after Quentin's death—and went to bed early and read, as was his custom.

The devoted James Amos, who had been chief butler at the White House and thereafter moved to Sagamore to look after his beloved colonel, was asleep on a couch in TR's dressing room just in case he might be needed. He awoke shortly after midnight hearing sounds of heavy breathing and found TR apparently unconscious. He called the trained nurse and Mrs. Roosevelt. They telephoned the doctor, but by the time he arrived the end had come. When the doctor left, Mrs. Roosevelt, James Amos, and Charlie Lee, who had been coachman and later chauffeur, knelt by TR's bed and recited the Lord's Prayer. Two days later he was buried in Young's Memorial Cemetery overlooking Oyster Bay Harbor.

NOTES

CHAPTER I

(1) Santa Rosa, California, Press Democrat, April 14, 1909

CHAPTER II

(1) Wister, Owen: Roosevelt, The Story of a Friendship: p. 325
(2) Thayer, W. R.: Life of John Hay: II p. 352
(3) TR to R. M. Ferguson, August 2, 1894, Greenway Mss., Arizona Historical Society

CHAPTER III

(1) Greenway Mss., Arizona Historical Society
(2) Hagedorn, Hermann: The Roosevelt Family of Sagamore Hill: p. 194

CHAPTER IV

(1) Parsons, Frances Theodora: Perchance Some Day: p. 27
(2) Hagedorn, H.: Transcripts (in TRA Library)
(3) id.
(4) id.

CHAPTER V

(1) Garraty, John A.: Henry Cabot Lodge, A Biography: p. 87
(2) Theodore Roosevelt Encyclopedia, quoted from B. Hendrick, Life of Andrew Carnegie
(3) Root, Elihu: Miscellaneous Addresses: p. 92
(4) Thayer, W. R.: Life of John Hay: II p. 362
(5) Root, Elihu: op. cit. pp. 94–5
(6) White, William Allen: Autobiography: p. 297
(7) TR Letters: II p. 1171

(8) Cater, H. D.: Henry Adams and his Friends: p. 730
(9) Adams, Henry: Letters: II p. 365
(10) id. II p. 419
(11) id. II p. 433
(12) TR Letters: V p. 10
(13) id. V p. 229
(14) id. V p. 263

Chapter VI

(1) Wister, Owen: op. cit. p. 66
(2) Bishop, J. B.: Theodore Roosevelt and His Time: II p. 158
(3) id. II p. 144
(4) NR Diary, June 14, 1912
(5) White, W. A.: Autobiography: p. 501
(6) Abbott, Lawrence: Impressions of Theodore Roosevelt: p. 187
(7) id. pp. 183–4
(8) Puleston, W. D.: Biography of A. T. Mahan: p. 91
(9) id. p. 159
(10) Root, Elihu: Miscellaneous Addresses
(11) Grey of Falloden, Viscount: Recreation: pp. 34–5

Chapter VII

(1) TR Autobiography: p. 38
(2) id. p. 57
(3) Harbaugh, W. H.: Power and Responsibility: p. 15
(4) TR Autobiography: p. 136
(5) Wister, Owen: op. cit. p. 32
(6) Davis, O. K.: Released for Publication: p. 133
(7) Leary, J. J.: Talks with TR: p. 214
(8) Thompson, Charles W.: Presidents I Have Known: p. 117
(9) Riis, Jacob A.: Theodore Roosevelt the Citizen: p. 69
(10) Root, Elihu: Miscellaneous Addresses: p. 222
(11) Lodge, H. C.: Selections from the Correspondence of Theodore Roosevelt and H. C. Lodge: I p. 181
(12) Adams, Henry: Education: Chapter XXVIII

Chapter VIII

(1) Mowry, G. E.: Theodore Roosevelt and the Progressive Movement: p. 131
(2) Harbaugh, W. H. op. cit. p. 441
(3) Thayer, W. R.: Theodore Roosevelt: p. 354
(4) TR Letters: VII p. 469
(5) id. VII p. 479
(6) Thayer, W. R.: Theodore Roosevelt: p. 333

(7) Mowry, G. E. op. cit. p. 236
(8) id. p. 239
(9) id. p. 239
(10) id. pp. 239–240
(11) id.

CHAPTER IX

(1) Harbaugh, W. H. op. cit. p. 428
(2) Lewis, W. D.: Life of Theodore Roosevelt: p. 369
(3) id. p. 370
(4) NR Diary
(5) Putnam, C.: Theodore Roosevelt, Vol. I: p. 467

CHAPTER X

(1) TR Letters: VII p. 797
(2) TR Autobiography: pp. 88–9
(3) id. p. 426
(4) id.
(5) Faulkner, H. U.: The Quest for Social Justice: p. 82
(6) TR Autobiography: p. 491
(7) id. p. 94
(8) TR Letters: VIII p. 922

CHAPTER XII

(1) Pinchot, Gifford: Breaking New Ground: p. 331
(2) id. p. 326
(3) TR Autobiography: p. 430
(4) Hays, Samuel P.: Conservation and the Gospel of Efficiency: p. 131
(5) Pringle, Henry F.: Theodore Roosevelt, A Biography: p. 105

CHAPTER XIII

(1) TR Letters: I p. 607
(2) Einstein, Lewis: Roosevelt: His Mind in Action: p. 127
(3) TR Letters: II p. 1185
(4) Bemis, Samuel F.: A Diplomatic History of the United States: pp. 509–510
(5) TR Letters: II p. 1192
(6) id. II pp. 1186–7, footnote
(7) Bemis, Samuel F.: op. cit. p. 513
(8) Farrand, Max: Memorandum conversation with TR and A. C. Coolidge, now in Henry C. Huntington Library
(9) id.
(10) Bemis, Samuel F.: op. cit. p. 515
(11) Bishop, J. B. op. cit. I pp. 308–9
(12) id. I p. 305

(13) TR Letters: V pp. 220–1
(14) Einstein, Lewis: op. cit. pp. 146–7

Chapter XIV

(1) Oliver, F. S.: Ordeal by Battle: p. 333
(2) Taylor, Life of A. T. Mahan: p. 277 (footnote)
(3) Link, A. S.: Wilson: II p. 278–9
(4) TR Letters: VII pp. 810–1
(5) id. VIII p. 823
(6) id.
(7) TR: America and the World War: pp. 250–1
(8) TR Letters: VIII p. 1150
(9) Link, op. cit. IV p. 334
(10) Link, op. cit.: III pp. 356–7
(11) TR: Encyclopedia: p. 319
(12) Link, op. cit. III p. 380
(13) id. III p. 384
(14) id. III p. 382
(15) id. III p. 401

Chapter XV

(1) Washburn, Charles G.: Theodore Roosevelt, the Logic of His Career: pp. 105–8
(2) TR Letters: IV p. 1178
(3) Oliver, F. S.: op. cit. p. 37
(4) id. p. 261
(5) id. p. 298
(6) id. p. 298
(7) id. p. 315
(8) Harbaugh, W. H.: op. cit.: p. 473
(9) Historical Statistics of the U.S.: p. 718
(10) TR: America and the World War: pp. 252–3
(11) TR: Fear God and Take Your Own Part: p. 39
(12) id. p. 126
(13) id. p. 200
(14) Hagedorn, H.: Leonard Wood: a Biography: II p. 171
(15) Perry, Ralph Barton: The Plattsburg Movement: p. 262
(16) Hagedorn, H.: Leonard Wood; a Biography: I p. 203
(17) Morison, S. E.: Oxford History of the United States: p. 852
(18) Stimson, H. L. and Bundy, McGeorge: On Active Service in Peace and War: pp. 92–3
(19) Hagedorn, H.: The Bugle that Woke America: p. 138
(20) TR to Ethel Roosevelt Derby, August 13, 1918; E. R. Derby Mss.

DRAMATIS PERSONAE

Adams, Henry: 1838–1918. Historian and socialite.
Aldrich, Nelson W.: 1841–1915. Senator and Republican leader.
Bacon, Robert: 1860–1919. Secretary of State; Ambassador to France.
Barnes, William, Jr.: 1866–1930. Republican leader in New York.
Bigelow, John: 1817–1911. Diplomat and journalist.
Borah, William E.: 1865–1940. U. S. Senator from Idaho.
Bryan, William Jennings: 1860–1925; Secretary of State, 1913–1915.
Bryce, Viscount James: 1838–1922. Author; Ambassador to the U. S., 1907–1913.
Bunau-Varilla, Philippe: 1860–1940. French engineer and Panamanian diplomat.
Burroughs, John: 1837–1921. Naturalist.
Butler, Nicholas M.: 1862–1947. Educator; Republican leader.
Carow, Edith K.: 1861–1948. Second wife of Theodore Roosevelt.
Chanler, Winthrop: Classmate and close friend of TR.
Choate, Joseph H.: 1832–1917. Ambassador to Great Britain, 1899–1905.
Coolidge, Archibald Cary: 1866–1928. Historian and diplomat.
Cowles, William Sheffield: 1846–1923. Naval officer; married Anna Roosevelt, elder sister of TR.
Depew, Chauncey M.: 1834–1928. U. S. Senator and political leader.
Derby, Ethel Roosevelt: 1891– . Second daughter of TR.
Dunne, Finley Peter: 1867–1936. "Mr. Dooley."
Einstein, Lewis: 1877–1949. Diplomat and author.
Garfield, James R.: 1865–1950. Conservationist and political leader.
Hadley, Herbert S.: 1872–1927. Governor of Missouri.
Hagedorn, Hermann: 1882–1964. Author of numerous books about TR.
Hanna, Marcus Alonzo: 1837–1904. U. S. Senator from Ohio; Republican leader.
Hay, John: 1838–1905. Private secretary to President Lincoln; Secretary of State, 1898–1905.

Holleben, Von: German Ambassador to the U. S., 1902–1903.

Hughes, Charles Evans: 1862–1948. Republican nominee for President, 1916; Secretary of State, 1921–1925; Chief Justice U. S. Supreme Court, 1930–1941.

Johnson, Hiram W.: 1866–1945. Governor of California, 1911–1917; nominee for Vice-President on Progressive Party ticket, 1912; U. S. Senator, 1917–1945.

Jusserand, Jules: 1855–1932. French Ambassador to U. S., 1902–1925.

Leary, John J.: 1874–1944. Journalist (successively with *New York Herald*, *Tribune*, and *World*).

Lee, Alice Hathaway: 1861–1884. First wife of TR.

Lee, Arthur H., Viscount Lee of Fareham: 1868–1944. English political leader; close personal friend of TR.

Lewis, William Draper: 1867–1949. Lawyer, author, biographer of TR.

Lodge, Henry Cabot: 1850–1924. U. S. Senator from Massachusetts; close friend and adviser of TR.

Longworth, Nicholas: 1869–1931. Member of Congress; Speaker of the House; husband of Alice Lee Roosevelt.

Mahan, Alfred Thayer: 1840–1914. Naval officer and author of *The Influence of Sea Power on History*.

Muensterberg, Hugo: 1863–1916. German propagandist in U. S.

Munsey, Frank A.: 1854–1925. Newspaper publisher; active supporter of Progressive Party.

Murdock, Victor: 1871–1945. Kansas Congressman and publisher; Progressive Party leader.

Oliver, Frederick Scott: 1864–1934. British author and historian.

Perkins, George W.: 1862–1920. Financier; treasurer of Progressive Party.

Pinchot, Gifford: 1865–1946. Forester; conservationist; leader in Progressive Party; close friend of TR.

Platt, Thomas C.: 1833–1910. U. S. Senator from New York; Republican leader.

Reid, Whitelaw: 1837–1912. Owner *New York Tribune;* U. S. Ambassador to Great Britain, 1905–1912.

Rhodes, James Ford: 1848–1927. Historian; brother-in-law of Mark Hanna.

Riis, Jacob A.: 1849–1914. Journalist; author; reformer.

Root, Elihu: 1845–1937. Secretary of State, 1905–1909; U. S. Senator, 1909–1915; Chairman Republican National Convention, 1912.

Speck von Sternburg, Hermann: 1852–1908. German Ambassador to U. S., 1903–1908; close friend of TR.

Spring-Rice, Sir Cecil Arthur: 1859–1918. Best man at TR's wedding to Edith Carow, 1886; British Ambassador to U. S., 1913–1918.

Stimson, Henry L.: 1867–1950. Candidate for Governor of New York,

1910; Secretary of War, 1911–1913; Secretary of State, 1929–1933; Secretary of War, 1940–1945.

Taft, William Howard: 1857–1930. Secretary of War, 1904–1908; President, 1909–1913; Chief Justice, U. S. Supreme Court, 1921–1930.

Thayer, William Roscoe: 1859–1923. Author and historian; biographer of TR.

Thompson, Charles Willis: 1871–1946. Journalist and author; staff member, *New York Times*.

Trevelyan, Sir George Otto: 1838–1928. British historian; nephew of T. B. Macaulay; friend and correspondent of TR.

Turner, Frederick Jackson: 1861–1932. Historian; author of *The Influence of the Frontier on American History*.

Washburn, Charles G.: 1857–1928. Member of Congress; author (including a brief biography of TR); Harvard classmate of TR.

White, Henry: 1850–1927. Diplomatist; close friend and adviser of TR.

White, William Allen: 1868–1944. Journalist; ardent progressive.

Wister, Owen: 1860–1938. Author (*The Virginian*) and close friend of TR.

Wood, Leonard: 1860–1927. Army officer, Colonel of Rough Riders, 1898; Chief of Staff, U. S., 1910–1914; organizer of "Plattsburg" training camps.

INDEX

INDEX

INDEX

INDEX

INDEX

INDEX